1980s Project Studies/Council on Foreign Relations

STUDIES AVAILABLE

ALTERNATIVES TO MONETARY DISORDER
Studies by Fred Hirsch and Michael W. Doyle and by Edward L. Morse

NUCLEAR PROLIFERATION:
Motivations, Capabilities, and Strategies for Control
Studies by Ted Greenwood and by Harold A. Feiveson and Theodore B. Taylor

INTERNATIONAL DISASTER RELIEF:
Toward a Responsive System
Stephen Green

CHINA'S FUTURE:
Foreign Policy and Economic Development in the Post-Mao Era
Studies by Allen S. Whiting and Robert F. Dernberger

STUDIES FORTHCOMING

Some 25 additional volumes of the 1980s Project will be appearing in the course of the next year or two. Most will contain independent but related studies concerning issues of potentially great importance in the next decade and beyond, such as the control of strategic weaponry, resource management, terrorism, relations between the developing and developed societies, and the world market in conventional arms, among many others. Additionally, a number of volumes will be devoted to particular regions of the world, concentrating especially on political and economic development trends outside the industrialized West.

Alternatives to Monetary Disorder

Alternatives to Monetary Disorder

FRED HIRSCH

MICHAEL W. DOYLE

EDWARD L. MORSE

1980s Project/Council on Foreign Relations

McGRAW-HILL BOOK COMPANY

New York   St. Louis   San Francisco
Auckland   Bogotá   Düsseldorf   Johannesburg   London   Madrid
Mexico   Montreal   New Delhi   Panama   Paris   São Paulo
Singapore   Sydney   Tokyo   Toronto

The Council on Foreign Relations, Inc. is a nonprofit and nonpartisan organization devoted to promoting improved understanding of international affairs through the free exchange of ideas. Its membership of about 1,700 persons throughout the United States is made up of individuals with special interest and experience in international affairs. The Council has no affiliation with and receives no funding from the United States government.

The Council publishes the quarterly journal *Foreign Affairs* and, from time to time, books and monographs which in the judgment of the Council's Committee on Studies are responsible treatments of significant international topics worthy of presentation to the public. The 1980s Project is a research effort of the Council; as such, 1980s Project Studies have been similarly reviewed through procedures of the Committee on Studies. As in the case of all Council publications, statements of fact and expressions of opinion contained in 1980s Project Studies are the sole responsibility of their authors.

The editor of this book was Michael Schwarz for the Council on Foreign Relations. Thomas Quinn and Michael Hennelly were the editors for McGraw-Hill Book Company. Christopher Simon was the designer and Milton J. Heiberg supervised the production. This book was set in Times Roman by Creative Book Services, Inc.

Printed and bound by R. R. Donnelley & Sons.

Library of Congress Cataloging in Publication Data

Hirsch, Fred.
Alternatives to monetary disorder.

(1980's project/Council on Foreign Relations)
Bibliography: p.
Includes index.
1. International finance. 2. International
economic relations. I. Doyle, Michael W., joint author.
II. Morse, Edward L., joint author. III. Title.
IV. Series: Council on Foreign Relations. 1980's
project/Council on Foreign Relations.
HG3881.H498   332.4'5   77-436
ISBN 0-07-029046-6
ISBN 0-07-029047-4 pł

1 2 3 4 5 6 7 8 9 RRDRRD 7 0 9 8 7

Contents

Foreword: The 1980s Project

The essays in this volume explore the nature of economic arrangements among nations that would be desirable during the next decade or two and the relationship between the monetary system and other aspects of international politics. They are part of a stream of studies to be produced in the course of the 1980s Project of the Council on Foreign Relations, each of which analyzes an issue or set of issues that is likely to be of international concern during the next 10 to 20 years.

The ambitious purpose of the 1980s Project is to examine important political and economic problems not only individually but in relationship to one another. Some studies or books produced by the Project will primarily emphasize the interrelationship of issues. In the case of other, more specifically focused studies, a considerable effort has been made to write, review, and criticize them in the context of more general Project work. Each Project study is thus capable of standing on its own; at the same time it has been shaped by a broader perspective.

The 1980s Project had its origins in the widely held recognition that many of the assumptions, policies, and institutions that have characterized international relations during the past 30 years are inadequate to the demands of today and foreseeable demands of the period between now and 1990 or so. Over the course of the next decade, substantial adaptation of institutions and behavior will be needed to respond to the changed circumstances of the 1980s and beyond. The Project seeks to identify those future conditions and the kinds of adaptation they might require. It is not the Project's purpose to arrive at a single or exclusive set of goals. Nor does it focus upon the foreign policy or national interests of the United States alone. Instead, it seeks to identify goals that are compatible with the perceived interests of most states, despite differences in ideology and in level of economic development.

The published products of the Project are aimed at a broad readership, including policy makers and potential policy makers and those who would influence the policy-making process, but confined to no single nation or region. The authors of Project studies were therefore asked to remain mindful of interests broader than those of any one society and to take fully into account the likely realities of domestic politics in the principal societies involved. All those who have worked in the Project, however, have tried not to be captives of the status quo; they have sought to question the inevitability of existing patterns of thought and behavior that restrain desirable change and to look for ways in which those patterns might in time be altered or their consequences mitigated.

The 1980s Project is at once a series of separate attacks upon a number of urgent and potentially urgent international problems and also a collective effort, involving a substantial number of persons in the United States and abroad, to bring those separate approaches to bear upon one another and to suggest the kinds of choices that might be made among them. The Project involves more than 300 participants. A small central staff and a steering Coordinating Group have worked to define the questions and to assess the compatibility of policy prescriptions. Nearly 100 authors, from more than a dozen countries, have been at work on separate studies. Ten working groups of specialists and generalists have been convened to subject the Project's studies to critical scrutiny and to help in the process of identifying interrelationships among them.

The 1980s Project is the largest single research and studies effort the Council on Foreign Relations has undertaken in its 55-year history, comparable in conception only to a major study of the postwar world, the War and Peace Studies, undertaken by the Council during the Second World War. At that time, the impetus to the effort was the discontinuity caused by worldwide conflict and the visible and inescapable need to rethink, replace, and supplement many of the features of the international system that had prevailed before the war. The discontinuities in today's world are less obvious and, even when occasionally quite visible—as in the abandonment of gold convertibility and fixed monetary parities—only briefly command the spotlight of public attention. That new institutions and patterns of behavior are needed in many areas is widely acknowledged, but the sense of need is less urgent—existing institutions have not for the most part dramatically failed and collapsed. The tendency, therefore, is to make do with outmoded arrangements and to improvise rather than to undertake a basic analysis of the problems that lie before us and of the demands that those problems will place upon all nations.

The 1980s Project is based upon the belief that serious effort and integrated forethought can contribute—indeed, are indispensable—to progress in the next decade toward a more humane, peaceful, productive, and just world. And it rests upon the hope that participants in its deliberations and readers of Project publications—whether or not they agree with an author's point of view—may be helped to think more informedly about the opportunities and the dangers that lie ahead and the consequences of various possible courses of future action.

The 1980s Project has been made possible by generous grants from the Ford Foundation, the Lilly Endowment, the Andrew W. Mellon Foundation, the Rockefeller Foundation, and the German Marshall Fund of the United States. Neither the Council on Foreign Relations nor any of those foundations is responsible for statements of fact and expressions of opinion contained in publications of the 1980s Project; they are the sole responsibility of the individual authors under whose names they appear. But the Council on Foreign Relations and the staff of the 1980s Project take great pleasure in placing those publications before a wide readership both in the United States and abroad.

Richard H. Ullman
Director, the 1980s Project

During 1975 and 1976, ten Working Groups met to explore major international issues and to subject initial drafts of 1980s Project studies to critical review. Those who chaired Project Working Groups were:

Cyrus R. Vance, Working Group on Nuclear Weapons and Other Weapons of Mass Destruction

Leslie H. Gelb, Working Group on Armed Conflict

Roger Fisher, Working Group on Transnational Violence and Subversion

Rev. Theodore M. Hesburgh, Working Group on Human Rights

Joseph S. Nye, Jr., Working Group on the Political Economy of North-South Relations

Harold Van B. Cleveland, Working Group on Macroeconomic Policies and International Monetary Relations

Lawrence C. McQuade, Working Group on Principles of International Trade

William Diebold, Jr., Working Group on Multinational Enterprises

Eugene B. Skolnikoff, Working Group on the Environment, the Global Commons, and Economic Growth

Miriam Camps, Working Group on Industrial Policy

The members of the 1980s Project staff are:

Miriam Camps　　　　　*Catherine Gwin*
William Diebold, Jr.　　*Roger Hansen*
David Gompert　　　　*Edward L. Morse*
Richard H. Ullman (Director)

The Committee on Studies of the Board of Directors of the Council on Foreign Relations was the governing body of the 1980s Project. The Committee's members as of December 31, 1976 were:

W. Michael Blumenthal Walter J. Levy
Zbigniew Brzezinski Joseph S. Nye, Jr.
Robert A. Charpie Robert V. Roosa
Richard N. Cooper Carroll L. Wilson
James A. Perkins (Chairman)

The Coordinating Group of the 1980s Project had a central advisory role in the work of the Project. Its members as of December 31, 1976 were:

W. Michael Blumenthal Theodore R. Marmor
Richard N. Cooper Ali Mazrui
Carlos F. Diaz-Alejandro Joseph S. Nye, Jr.
Richard A. Falk Michael O'Neill
Edward K. Hamilton Marshall D. Shulman
Stanley Hoffman Stephen Stamas
Samuel P. Huntington Fritz Stern
Gordon J. MacDonald Allen S. Whiting
Bruce K. MacLaury
Bayless Manning (Chairman)

Alternatives to Monetary Disorder

Introduction: Money and the Structure of International Politics

William Diebold, Jr.

Since the middle of the 1960s the world has been remaking its international monetary system. First, shifting relations between the United States and the other leading industrial nations of the Western world brought strains, repairs, and partial reform. In 1971 unilateral action by the United States drastically altered the central role of the dollar. The sharp rise in oil prices in 1973 brought new shocks. By 1976 the Articles of Agreement of the International Monetary Fund had been amended to legitimize, ex post facto, the practice of letting the foreign value of currencies fluctuate, which was in sharp contrast to the ideal of fixed exchange rates that had been agreed on at Bretton Woods, New Hampshire in 1944.

But the unwillingness of most governments to accept complete flexibility sharply posed once more the question whether governments could agree on new international rules. In the late 1970s it was less clear than it had been for decades whether a monetary system would be widely accepted if only a few key governments made the important decisions, or whether more nations would have to play a significant part.

Although much of the trouble with the monetary system was linked to changes in the world economy, political strands ran through the process. Charles de Gaulle thought that the United States government had the "exorbitant privilege" of printing money that the rest of the world had to accept and so was free to finance whatever foreign policy it wanted to pursue. But to many

Americans, that same monetary system created an artificial value for the dollar which damaged the American economy and permitted European nations and Japan to avoid carrying their fair share of the economic burdens of the world.

Weak and poor countries have always felt themselves excluded from any influence over the monetary system because of the concentration of power and wealth in a few great financial centers of the industrial world. But when the oil-exporting countries suddenly became the owners of large foreign exchange balances, Europeans, Americans, and Japanese feared that the movement of these funds from country to country would both create imbalances within the monetary system and put great pressure on the industrial countries to conform to the owners' views of foreign policy.

These and many other events contribute to the monetary problems of today. But for the 1980s Project the key questions are, What kind of international monetary system should the world be trying to create for the future? Ought it be a modified version of what we have known or something radically different? If different, in what respects?

One way of answering these questions is to examine in detail the operating features of a monetary system: whether exchange rates are mostly fixed or mostly flexible; whether gold, dollars, or some other kind of assets are chosen as national monetary reserves; how a country can finance its balance of payments deficits; and so on. These are important issues on which there is already a large and rich literature. There have been many prescriptions for alternative systems, modifications, repairs, and restoratives. They range from eclectic mosaics and single-minded panaceas to some rather Rube Goldberg–like devices that inspire confidence in some and alarm in others.

Instead of making further studies of this sort, the 1980s Project has adopted a different approach. This decision stems in part from a conclusion reached by Miriam Camps as a result of her work which paved the way for the Project. She pointed out that "decisions on international monetary arrangements raise in an inescapable way basic political and social questions. Behind the jargon of crawling pegs, fixed rates, optimum currency areas, adjustment process, and all the rest are some very basic questions which are more often evaded than asked."[1] The questions have been asked more and more frequently in the last few years, but further exploration remains crucial to discussion of what the world of the 1980s ought to be like. There is, however, a still more explicit need to relate the monetary system to the international system as a whole, especially to the shifting patterns of economic and political strengths and weaknesses in the world. This is the focus of the two essays in this volume.

The approaches of these studies are different but complementary. Fred Hirsch and Michael W. Doyle analyze the controversies of recent years and then work out what they believe is a reasonable arrangement that would both satisfy the needs (and some of the demands) of developing countries and also assure efficient economic performance. Edward L. Morse compares four different "regimes"—alternate ways in which the international monetary system might be organized. He shows what each would require—or tend to produce—in terms of international relations generally and finally argues the merits of the arrangement he prefers, which resembles the formula of Hirsch and Doyle.

Naturally the two papers do not ignore the relation of monetary issues to the rest of the international economy. Morse says a good deal about different kinds of trading relations and different degrees and patterns of economic cooperation among countries that would be entailed in alternative regimes. Hirsch and Doyle treat at length trade, investment, and the financing of development when they explain both the sources of trouble and the possibilities of finding compromise formulas for a monetary system. In other parts of its work, the 1980s Project examines many economic issues that are affected by the monetary questions discussed in these pages. Quite a few closely related issues are addressed directly in essays on the international dimensions of the conduct of national economic policies and on the ways resources flow—or might flow—between rich and poor countries.

[1]Miriam Camps, *The Management of Interdependence: A Preliminary View,* Council on Foreign Relations, Inc., New York, 1974, p. 55.

Studies of East-West relations and the future position of the Communist countries in the world economy have raised still more unanswered questions.

Mostly, though, these two papers are about the place of money in the international system as a whole. Morse stresses the difficulties stemming from the increased complexity of international relations and the diversity among countries. He says, "the evolution of the international monetary order will tend to parallel the evolution of the structure of international society as a whole." His four regimes show very clearly how different relations between countries would be if, for example, a world central bank dominated the monetary system than if, instead, monetary arrangements enabled every country to exercise maximum freedom at home and do no more than the minimum necessary to keep from having major trouble abroad. Monetary blocs cannot exist without affecting other relations among members and nonmembers of blocs. Questions about what combinations of countries are essential (or helpful) for what purposes are as central and as troublesome as those about what happens if certain issues are linked or not linked with monetary questions.

These matters are systematically analyzed by Hirsch and Doyle in terms of the "politicization" of monetary issues. It may come as a surprise to some people to hear that anyone ever thought that international monetary relations were "economic" in some sense that was not also "political," but a great deal has been written as if that were so. Hirsch and Doyle, however, explain quite carefully the several senses in which international monetary issues are now more politicized than they were for many years during which the Bretton Woods arrangements were not seriously called into question. This politicization predates the problems of the Organization of Petroleum Exporting Countries (OPEC), petrodollars, and the Group of 77—the negotiating bloc of the developing countries as a whole. Nevertheless, there is now an inescapable intermixture of the monetary issue with what are called "North-South issues"—questions on the relationships between the developed and developing nations—that play a major part in the work of the 1980s Project.

As both papers make clear, it is not enough simply to find ways

4

of being "fair" to new nations and those that for other reasons had no voice in drawing up the Bretton Woods rules. More places at the table and more recognition of new wealth and power are undoubtedly needed. But are there any formulas that can accurately—and acceptably—measure the relevant combination of power, responsibility, sovereignty, and a country's stake in the system? Morse shows the great differences among the political compromises and blends of values that would be needed for different monetary regimes. Hirsch and Doyle make many suggestions about the variety of factors that should be considered in striking a balance.

Both papers come out in much the same place. The authors see no way of escaping the conclusion that since the major industrial nations play such a large part in the world economy, they must also be at the center of an efficient monetary system. Hirsch, Doyle, and Morse all want a high degree of cooperation among nations and believe that to get it there has to be some concentration of power and some broadening of the past concentration. The United States and the dollar are not to play the central part they did before. A number of countries are to be drawn in, though not, for the most part, to the very center of money management. Both papers recognize that for a two- (or three-) tiered system to be made acceptable to those on the lower tiers, the monetary system and arrangements connected with it have to show more clearly than in the past how they serve the interests of these countries.

The complex and delicate ways in which the authors of these studies hope to achieve these balances have to be read in their own words at the end of their arguments, not in crude advance summaries. There is little doubt, though, that it is on these matters that the largest disagreements will arise. Some observers will contend that since an efficient monetary system in fact requires the cooperation of only a few major industrial countries, these governments should not get too embroiled in the need to placate weaker countries by giving them a nominal status that belies their true importance, but instead should get on with the business of agreeing among themselves on the most important issues. At the other end of the spectrum will be those who would give greater weight to more egalitarian ideas, denounce concentrated power, and stress wider participation even at the cost of efficiency in the monetary system. In between will be people who would choose different mixes of factors from those of the authors—to whom they would be indebted for many ideas.

As in all analyses of changing situations, a time factor is involved. This creates difficulties for writers in the 1980s Project. They have to look far ahead and escape the constraints of worrying about what is likely to be acceptable to governments and electorates in the next few years. But they must also be in some sense realistic about what kinds of arrangements might be worked out over time. Hirsch, Doyle, and Morse distinguish clearly between the emphasis of their prescriptions and the compromise arrangements that would probably be necessary. These efforts underline some of the difficulties of their approaches. For example, it would be wrong to think of the measures Hirsch and Doyle call "sweeteners" as lollipops for the well-behaved. They ought to be thought of as ingredients that make the mixture more palatable, even though one has to accept someone else's cooking. Seen that way, they alter the trade-offs that every government— including the rich and powerful—has to make. But sometimes the sweeteners *will* be seen as payoffs—one might as well say "bribes"—and when that happens, there is little doubt that the time will come when the recipients will ask for more and the old issues will have to be reopened.

Using a different vocabulary, Morse's fourth and preferred regime has to cope with the same problem. No doubt, if the system works to their advantage, many second-tier countries (they are not all LDCs) will find it acceptable, as most of the world did the Bretton Woods regime. Here we come to a question that runs through much of the 1980s work: Can any limited group of countries be expected, over time, to use their power for the benefit of others? Perhaps most people would say no, but the answer could be yes if those with power conceived their own interests to be sufficiently bound up with the satisfactory operation of the international system. Then what they would "give" to others would be what was needed to keep them engaged and to discourage them from using whatever power they had to disrupt matters. The authors pursue this question in enlightening discussions of the provision of public goods and of the question of whether a group of countries can provide the leadership the United States did in the 1940s and 1950s. But no approach can escape the time-bound element in the answer, and since performance can fulfill expectations for only so long, any solution will be eventually unstable. Perhaps it is enough to realize this and so to judge prescriptions by what they promise to do on a time scale roughly similar to that of the Bretton Woods system—say a quarter of a century.

There are further obstacles to be overcome. No consensus exists among the key industrial countries about what the monetary system should be. The differences that brought about the end of the Bretton Woods system were primarily differences among the United States, Western Europe, and Japan. Until the key countries in that group find common ground, there can be nothing as ambitious as Hirsch and Doyle or Morse would like to see. Perhaps, as Morse suggests, a "truce" would be initially sufficient if governments could agree that "damage limitation" does not extend to "beggar thy neighbor." But one feels that something more positive is called for.

Here again monetary issues intersect with much other work of the 1980s Project, and it would be foolish in this introductory note to try to say anything conclusive about cooperation among the main industrial countries. However, it is perhaps worth underlining that unless there is a good bit of real agreement within this group, a large number of the North-South issues will take on a different cast, and the building of a desirable global monetary system will hardly be possible. Unless the industrial countries can achieve by the 1980s a level of agreement that has eluded them for nearly a decade, some of the problems of relations between tiers and of the provision of public goods will hardly arise.

"Economically weaker partners see politicization as a potential route to equality," say Hirsch and Doyle. No doubt this is so, but if the result of politicization is that each country acts according to what its most narrowly nationalistic and mercantilistic people think are its real interests, will not the poor and weak come off worse than the rich and powerful? To be sure, in the era of OPEC one is not entirely certain who is rich and who is weak, but the prospect of finding out by testing can be costly to many people. Presumably the world as a whole loses if the monetary system breaks down. But it is hard to believe that distribution of the losses is the problem most people want to solve.

As these last few paragraphs suggest, it is much easier to suppose that things will go wrong than that they will go right. Governments that concentrate on the immediate negotiating position abroad or political pressures at home—and that means, of course, most governments most of the time—will have trouble pursuing the kinds of consistent and broadly conceived policies required to build a new monetary system and to keep it working in the long run. However, these requirements were met once before, and perhaps they can be met again. The authors of these papers are inclined to think so. One hopes they are right.

Politicization in the World Economy: Necessary Conditions for an International Economic Order

Fred Hirsch and Michael W. Doyle

ONE

Politics in the International Economy

THE DUAL PERSPECTIVE

A common thread that runs through diagnosis of current trends in the international economy is the theme of increasing politicization. Economic matters that were once dealt with at a technical level or left entirely to the outcome of market forces are increasingly the subject of international diplomacy. The leading economic powers of the noncommunist world have institutionalized the economic summit conference. An almost continuous series of conferences has brought together representatives of the developed countries, the less developed countries, and the oil-exporting countries to discuss problems of energy supply, raw materials, economic development, and international finance. These matters have hitherto been dealt with independently and in low key. It is now the overt aim of the developing world to link these issues. Beyond this, by elevating decisions to the highest political level, developing nations hope to substitute politicization for what they see as tacit acceptance of the status quo as it manifests itself through the operation of market forces and technical management.

The developing world, as challenger to today's balance and structure of political and economic power, sees increasing the explicit politicization of the international economy as an opportunity to forge a new international economic order more favorable to its interests. By contrast, in the view that dominates both

11

governmental attitudes and the main thrust of analytical discussion in the developed world, the focus is on the dangers of increased political friction and economic disruption that would result from the substitution of political decisions for market or technical influences. Western governments see politicization as a threat to both economic prosperity and political harmony. In their opinion, the containment and reversal of the trend toward increasing politicization are among the most urgent international problems of the next decade.

The trend toward increasing politicization in the world economy therefore appears in a dual perspective, and persons accustomed to one of the perspectives find it difficult to adjust to or even recognize the other. Associated with this dichotomy are differing interpretations of the meaning and consequences of politicization itself.

This paper seeks, in this section, to identify these differing notions of politicization. In the following sections, the paper argues that (1) there is indeed a present and prospective trend toward politicization in the international economy; but (2) the sources of this trend are partly obscured in the liberal perspective prevalent in the developed countries, particularly by the special environmental conditions associated with American dominance in the first two decades after World War II; so that (3) the conditions necessary for limiting and "taming" economic politicization, or "constitutionalizing" it, have not been fully identified. Drawing on both perspectives, the paper posits that politicization can simultaneously involve potential dangers for all and distributional gains for some. It follows that from a global standpoint, the objective of reducing politicization is unacceptable as a norm in itself unless accompanied by some compensation to those groups that would otherwise stand to gain from it.

No generally agreed upon definition of *politicization* in the context of international (or for that matter national) economic transactions has been developed. Current usage can be categorized as embracing four concepts of ascending order of strength and significance:

1. Politicization relates essentially to what is on the agendas of governments and to who within governments deals with eco-

nomic issues. In this case increased politicization refers to the fact that economic issues are more frequently than in the past dealt with at a higher political level, including summit meetings. Politicization here is merely what politicians do. The emphasis is on the *actors*—i.e., on the transfer of economic questions from purely economic agencies to higher, more general policy-making bodies.

2. Economic issues are not merely items on the agenda of politicians but are political issues in domestic politics. Increased exports can mean higher employment, just as higher levels of imports can, in the short run, mean higher unemployment. Politicians feel increasingly responsive to these economic fluctuations, since the economic welfare of the electorate influences sources of political support. The emphasis here is on *constituents*.

3. International economic issues are not only domestic political issues, but are consequently linked to other and "higher" aspects of national foreign policy. During the 1960s and early 1970s, for example, persistent American payments deficits and perceived impediments to the export of American agricultural products to Western Europe reduced United States domestic support for NATO commitments, especially the stationing of American troops in Germany. This form of politicization through the linkage of such otherwise disparate issues as security policy and trade policy thus affects the *process* of foreign policy and of foreign economic relations.

4. Finally, international economic relationships—whether or not they are seen as matters of governmental policy—can so constrain states' opportunities that not only autonomy but also effective sovereignty are lost. Governments lack control over the instruments of economic policy as well as over the outcome desired from using those instruments. This lack of control reflects a more general limitation of autonomy.[1] Thus politicization also refers to the consequences of international economic policies on the *structure* of relationships within which policies compete, actors act, and issues are raised.

[1]The meaning of these terms is discussed below.

Politicization, as has been seen, is also a normative concept. Thus these four different forms of economic politicization can be evaluated differently, according to the perspective from which they are viewed. Mainstream *liberal* thought—prevalent in the United States and most of the Western world—traditionally regards the politicization of economic issues as both an inefficient way to create and allocate wealth and a potentially destructive influence on harmonious relationships, both in domestic affairs and among nations. It therefore ought to be minimized. A corollary to this view is that politicization is an aberration from normal and desirable economic relationships at arm's length—i.e., largely removed—from government interference. The central political task, according to liberal thought, is thus essentially "constitutional"—it involves constructing an overarching framework for an international order as a way to make arbitrary day-to-day government intervention unnecessary. Such a constitutional order would allow economic influences to operate through market mechanisms in a smooth, certain, and unimpeded way.

Another normative approach that now has strong appeal in the developing world has its intellectual roots in *Marxist* and in *neo-mercantilist* thought. Unlike the mainstream liberal view—which regards political and economic relations as separate and separable—this approach sees political and economic relations as integral parts of each other. Especially when economic interchange involves partners of unequal size and position—e.g., the United States and Chile, France and Algeria, or the Soviet Union and Bulgaria—economic relations are seen as inevitably involving extra gains and advantages—or even political domination—for the larger economic power. Economically weaker partners see politicization as a potential route to equality. They thus welcome it not only as a raising to consciousness of the fundamental politics of economics but also as a way to change relations of dependence. The pervasiveness of these perceptions helps to explain the remarkable unity of the less developed countries in their demands for a new international economic order.

The kernel of the liberal approach is that politicization involves departures from the perceived norms of neutrality and harmony that characterize economic relationships in the market model in which government intervention is minimal. The key analytical grounding for this view is, in game-theoretic terms, the indeterminacy of any bargaining solution: each party has the incentive to adapt its behavior in order to reap the best bargain. This gives an incentive for "gaming" behavior, which is both inefficient and conducive to conflict. The ideal international economic order is therefore one in which states are restrained from exercising their potential bargaining power on specific transactions, for example by trying to manipulate tariffs and other fiscal or administrative regulatory devices to their own advantage. This ideal was the free-trade order of Cobden, never realized on a worldwide basis but approached in the third quarter of the nineteenth century. The antithesis was reached with the breakdown of the international economy in the 1930s, when protectionism became dominant and involved not merely the retaliatory escalation of tariffs but recourse to what were then new forms of political intervention restricting trade: quotas, exchange controls, bilateral trade discrimination, and—arguably—competitive exchange depreciation.

This unprecedented politicization of the international economy was seen by many observers—most notably including U.S. Secretary of State Cordell Hull—as an important element in the origins of World War II. Economic nationalism, it was believed, exacerbated political nationalism and led to the more frequent use of force to achieve national goals. Major efforts were therefore made, in planning for the postwar world, to establish a global constitutional framework that would provide safeguards against a perpetuation or recurrence of continuous political intrusions in world trade relations. These attempts acknowledged that restrictions on trade and payments could be removed only through deliberate organization. This view represented an important intellectual advance over the misapplied rationalism of the nineteenth-century Cobdenite free-traders.[2]

[2] For an early demonstration of why "some form of compulsion is necessary to ensure free trade," see Tibor Scitovsky, "A Reconsideration of the Theory of Tariffs," 1942, reproduced in *Readings in the Theory of International Trade,* American Economic Association, London, 1970, p. 389.

In the first two decades after World War II, the strategy of moving towards an economically integrated world economy on the basis of agreed international codes appeared to be successful. Restrictions on international trade and payments were markedly reduced; the code embodied in the international economic institutions—primarily the International Monetary Fund (IMF) and the General Agreement on Tariffs and Trade (GATT)—was a clear guiding influence. However, since the mid-1960s this progress has been halted and in important respects reversed. The international trade and payments code has become less influential and, in aspects such as exchange rate regulation, has broken down.

The GATT code of reciprocal trade liberalization on a nondiscriminatory basis has been challenged formally by the demands for special treatment of less developed countries in the United Nations Conference on Trade and Development (UNCTAD) program of action and informally by the impact of the European Economic Community's special discriminatory trade relations with associated members. The result has been the proliferation rather than the diminution of various preferential arrangements.

These impediments encountered by the liberal ideal are not surprising to persons in the less developed world and also in some developed states whose perspectives are Marxist or mercantilist. Politicization to them means an open challenging of political relationships previously only implicit in economic activities. The analytical basis for this challenge lies in the political roles embodied in economic relations, which are in principle twofold. First, economic exchange can always be used as a tool of political power through boycotts, bribery, and the manipulation of trade incentives. Second, economic relationships can operate on a more fundamental level, shaping the political-economic foundations of a weaker, less developed economy through the opportunity offered to it in the form of trade and finance. The weaker country in an economic relationship, like a weaker class, then becomes not just a group of assorted individuals but a particularized, isolated, and dependent participant in the world economy—e.g., a single crop exporter, an economy split into largely self-contained export and domestic sectors, or a "hewer of wood." Mercantilists see nations, as Marxists see classes, becoming alienated in the process of production and exchange.

These normative nationalistic concerns are far from new; they were eloquently addressed by Hamilton in his *Report on Manufactures* of 1790, in which he expressed the opposition of American nationalists to their country's assuming the role of a raw material exporter to Britain. Nationalists feared and opposed two aspects of this role: the tying of American economic development to the British economy and the growing dependence on Britain for goods vital to national defense. Friedrich List, inspired by Hamilton's observations of American trade policy, outlined in *American Political Economy* what he saw as the proper object for a developing country's commercial policy:

This object is not to gain matter, *in exchanging matter for matter*, as it is in individual and cosmopolitical [liberal] economy, and particularly in the trade of a merchant. But it is *to gain productive and political power* by means of exchange with other nations; or to prevent the depression of productive and political power, by restricting that exchange.[3]

At the earliest stages of development, a free-trade policy designed to encourage new commodities and techniques may be advantageous; but at later stages, and in order to develop a national culture and a national system of industry, protection will be needed to stimulate the growth of infant industries and avoid foreign-dominated dependence.

Transposing this analysis from nation to class, Marxism-Leninism provides similar guidelines for national development: The colonial bourgeoisie, nurtured in dependence, will initiate independent development through an anticolonial bourgeois revolution. Maoism, while stressing the revolutionary character of the necessary break from the international economy, adds that this development should and can be effected by a mobilized revolutionary peasantry.

These Marxian doctrines are plainly evident in the development strategies of the Second World of Russia, Eastern Europe,

[3]Friedrich List, *Outlines of American Political Economy*, S. Parker, Philadelphia, 1827, p. 18. Also in *National Gazette*, August 18–November 27, 1827.

and China. And in the First World, mercantilism inspired de Gaulle's challenge to the dominance of the dollar. Both these strands of thought find a place in the developmental programs and campaigns of Third World leaders in the postwar world. At the national level, the crude expression of this thinking is to be found in programs of import substitution, designed to reduce dependence upon foreign sources of supply, foreign markets, and foreign capital.

The limitations of this approach, notably in cutting off the national economy from the stimulus of the world market, have led to more ambitious programs for managing the allocation of resources and technology at the international level. The intellectual and organizational pioneer in this effort was Raul Prebisch, first in his work as secretary of the Economic Commission for Latin America and then as the driving spirit in the creation and first session of the United Nations Conference on Trade and Development. Prebisch's program was a bold attempt to reverse what he saw as a systematic bias toward adverse terms of trade between raw materials and industrial products. UNCTAD developed a comprehensive program aimed at reducing dependence and promoting development through the cooperation of Third World countries. Its organizational expression was the Group of 77, the coalition of developing countries formed at the first UNCTAD conference in 1964. Its substantive program, by embracing a wide front of trade and financial issues, involved a general increase in politicization. This included negotiation, through the management of supplies, of the price of raw materials produced by the less developed countries.

The UNCTAD program, which lay behind the 1975 resolution of the Seventh Special Session of the UN General Assembly calling for a new international economic order, includes a number of far-reaching extensions—and abrogations—of the existing international trading code. The most important such elements are the following:

- Commodity agreements designed both to transfer resources and to stabilize prices

- Preferential access to industrial markets for exports of developing countries
- Limitations on the activities of multinational companies
- Entrenchment of host countries' control over exploitation of natural resources

Other important elements in the proposed new international economic order—notably a major extension of aid, both in traditional forms and through such new international instruments as a link between reserve creation and allocation of special drawing rights—have important implications for developed countries but do not in themselves conflict with the established international trade and payments codes.

THE INTERNATIONAL ORDER AS A COLLECTIVE GOOD

While a new international economic order is being proclaimed by resolution, in fact the international order is disintegrating in the sense that no generally accepted and generally observed framework for national action in the fields of trade, payments, and foreign investment any longer exists. To be sure, the established body of rules continues to exert a major influence—notably in inhibiting the large industrial countries from raising tariffs and introducing import restrictions. An important inhibition that has put a high cost on any transgression of international obligations (as in the case of the United Kingdom in recent years) has been the fear of being cut off from sources of international loans. An additional influence has been the interest of particular groups within industrial countries in maintaining an open economy as a restraining pressure on the actions of their own governments: external necessity adds power to the elbow of domestic pressure groups concerned to limit the extent of government intervention. But the trend away from international consensus is clear.

The erosion of order in the international economic system in the mid-1970s, it must be admitted, has had to date generally mild, even benign, results. A major reason for this, and a happy contrast with the breakdown in international economic order in the 1930s, is that the post-World War II system has crumbled less because of major conflicts of interests and misunderstandings between the leading economic powers than because the system has been unable to cope with the new problems and new situations that have emerged, including the new demands of the weak but strident. Thus the system has broken down but the will to international cooperation has not. Cooperation of a fairly high order has in fact been evoked in the past few years at a number of crucial points:

- New official financing facilities designed to cope with the massive oil surplusses
- A major extension of IMF credit facilities for developing countries
- The continuance, and in some aspects intensification, of consultation on cyclical policy and exchange rate management among the leading countries of the Organization for Economic Cooperation and Development (OECD)

Since floating exchange rates became widely used in 1973, payments imbalances have been exceptionally large as a result of the oil surplusses, and no significant case of national policy conflict among exchange authorities has occurred. This is a considerable if negative tribute to the maintenance of informal international cooperation in this important sphere.

The uneasy question remains as to how much this continued basis of informal cooperation is a depleting legacy of the earlier established economic order and must therefore be realistically expected to atrophy as the grounding of a clear set of international rules is progressively weakened. Ad hoc cooperation in itself—devoid of the foundation of an established rule book or code—not only is limited in efficacy but also can exacerbate disorder in the system as a whole. Piecemeal bargains and deals among small groups may help solve particular problems but in sum are likely to result in incoherence leading to provocation and conflict. Bilateral agreements that are not extended to account for the interests of third parties are the most direct example. An associated danger is an impulse towards linkage of trade and other economic matters with extraneous political issues. For these reasons, a continued absence of an operational economic order in the 1980s threatens a more serious deterioration in the international economic system than is superficially apparent from experience in the first few years of the breakdown of the established order.

The drift towards an ad hoc basis of international cooperation therefore contains lurking dangers. By confining cooperation to the instances and occurrences in which it benefits only the parties concerned, ad hoc cooperation neglects the characteristic of social cooperation as a collective rather than a private good. This can be shown formally to produce less cooperation than each individual party would wish and would be prepared to pay for. Collective-goods analysis[4] has not usually been applied to the international economic framework in a formal way, but the approach brings out a number of necessary supporting conditions that are frequently lost sight of.

The essential characteristic of international economic relations in this context is that, in game-theoretic terms, they comprise a mixed-motive game. That is to say, international economic transactions can produce *both* joint gains for the parties concerned and a gain for one party at the expense of others; and most, though not all, attempts to capture these latter distributional gains will reduce the size of the available joint gain. Since in individual piecemeal transactions the benefits available to a particular party at the expense of other parties will often exceed its associated fear of a loss from a reduced joint gain, the social optimizing condition requires that restraints on pursuit of distributional gains must be embodied in a constitutional framework or order; they cannot be expected to be adequately applied in piecemeal agreements.[5]

[4]The *locus classicus* is Mancur Olson, *The Logic of Collective Action,* Harvard University Press, Cambridge, Mass., 1965, 1971.

[5]The reason is that the full benefits from such restraints depend on reactions by other parties, and these reactions will depend in only a small and often peripheral part on the actions of the country concerned; they will depend overwhelmingly on the actions of other countries. Thus each "provocative"

Thus the general significance of the rules and procedures of the GATT has been summarized as recognition by all adherents that "national actions influencing international trade were matters of *mutual* concern, not merely, as before World War II, matters of purely domestic policy."[6] The same recognition of the mutuality of national action affecting the exchange rate and international payments underlies the articles of agreement of the IMF. In both organizations, member countries agree at the constitutional level to two basic kinds of limitations on their freedom of action. The first limitation involves adherence to a set of rules or guidelines on the form of the trade and payments regime (obligations to avoid import quotas except in specified circumstances, the binding of tariffs, avoidance of restrictions on current payments, etc.). The second limitation operates through the general obligation for nondiscrimination or equal treatment among all member countries. This obligation, as Cooper points out, has the important effect of sealing off trade and payments bargaining from other aspects of national foreign policy. If country A's trade concession to country B has to be extended to countries C, D, etc., it will normally be an inefficient instrument of leverage over country B.[7] The codes of the international economic organizations involve a depoliticization of trade and payments issues in the particular sense of removing or at least greatly diminishing the role of trade and payments issues in national foreign policy bargaining.

Trade issues and money issues, in Cooper's characterization, were kept on their own tracks in this way. It has been the erosion of this compartmentalization in the early 1970s, and the consequential increased linkage of trade and monetary issues both with

---

action produces a minor impact on the party undertaking it (the private-good element). This is the basis for the self-denying code or self-imposed set of obligations that is characteristic of collective action in organizations extending from the private club to the international community of nations.

[6]Richard N. Cooper, "Trade Policy Is Foreign Policy," *Foreign Policy*, Winter 1972–1973, p. 20.

[7]Normally, because in exceptional cases in which two countries have a mutual trade interest that is shared only peripherally by others, their obligation to extend trade concessions multilaterally is of minor significance in the bilateral bargain.

one another and with wider aspects of foreign policy, that has constituted increased politicization in the international economy in the sense that this term is most frequently used by liberal analysts and commentators. From this perspective, the normative issue of policy is typically put in the following way: What steps can be taken to check and contain increasing politicization of this kind? What are the terms of a political truce in the international economic arena?

While this is probably the central issue for the 1980s in international economic relations, it is seen in false perspective if the concept of politicization is confined to the process level. For depoliticization, or "track separation" at this level, itself rests on particular political foundations at what we have called the constitutional level. The issue is crucial, because the relationship is fundamentally an inverse one—establishment of a constitution, or "meta"politicization, being a condition of depoliticization at the process level.

It is at this level of metapoliticization that the liberal and Marxist-mercantilist perspectives intersect. The liberal would agree that economic relationships always rest on political foundations—on the provision of rules and order by constitutional political bargains. The liberal then would argue that apolitical economics begins from this point. The Marxist-mercantilist, in contrast, sees the politico-economic constitution as a product of imposition rather than bargain and the interchanges that follow as more a product of politico-economic coercion than a maximization of aggregated individual welfare.[8] The significance of these

[8]An early proponent of the modern neo-mercantilist position was E. H. Carr, in his attack on the notion of free trade as a universalistic interest as distinct from one serving the political and economic interests of the dominant power, Great Britain. E. H. Carr, *The Twenty Years' Crisis, 1919–1939,* Macmillan, New York, 1939.

For a more recent development of this theme extended to the Pax Americana, see in particular Robert Gilpin, "The Politics of Transnational Economic Relations," *International Organization,* Summer 1971. See also David P. Calleo and Benjamin M. Rowland, *America and the World Political Economy,* University of Indiana Press, Bloomington, Ind., 1973. For a contemporary Marxist interpretation, see Harry Magdoff, *The Age of Imperialism,* Monthly Review Press, New York, 1966.

perceptions for the current state of the politico-economic international order, and for prospects over the next few years, can be brought into clearer focus by a brief interpretation of how the post-World War II constitutional order was created and developed.

TWO

The Basis of the Postwar Economic Order

ORIGINS OF THE BRETTON WOODS SYSTEM

Following World War II, the United States tried to establish a global order to secure an international economy based on open access and nondiscrimination. This goal reflected the Cobdenite faith that free trade would provide the basis for peace and that commercial relations would substitute for political relations among states.[9] U.S. Secretary of State Cordell Hull masterminded the first moves toward negotiated free trade through the reciprocal trade agreements initiated in 1934. But Hull's free-trade ideology would not have triumphed without propitious circumstances. At the end of World War II, the United States was the dominant economy in a world checkered with trade restrictions and discriminatory trade and payments arrangements that had their base in the 1930s and had been greatly extended during the war itself. These circumstances made a major international effort toward freer and less discriminatory trade and payments an obvious United States national interest.

The liberal literature interprets the United States drive for multilateralism as primarily an American recognition of the global benefits to be gained by freer trade and investment—requiring, consequentially, American resources and cooperative leadership to contain nationalistic interests that might threaten a free-trade

[9]Gilpin, "Transnational Economic Relations."

order. In addition, some liberal interpreters would argue that American leadership was needed to overcome culturally based antipathies of certain European nations—notably France—to those benefits.[10] The ending of the liberal postwar era in the late 1960s and early 1970s is then attributed to an unfortunate resurgence of narrow nationalism among the European states and the Third World.

In contrast, Marxist and neo-mercantilist or Gaullist literature interpret the postwar order as a product of the neoimperial imposition by the United States of its national interest upon Europe and the Third World.[11] Consequently, the strains in the postwar order reflect these governments' dissatisfaction with a global regime inimical to their interests and their increased ability to assert these interests through increased political and economic strength.

The Marxist-mercantilist perspective neglects the possible congruence—or at least overlap—of interests. Specifically, it leaves no room for what Kindleberger has called the "leadership" function in the international economy—the function of entrepreneur of the collective good of the international economic order that yields some benefits for all. The common- or collective-good element is in outlets for trade and investment and in stable monetary relations between the economies of Europe and the Third World and the economy of the United States.

But the liberal perspective correspondingly neglects the irony that hegemony is present in a cooperative system led by a dominant economy. Even though the entrepreneur of the collective good may provide benefits for all, those benefits may be of vastly different size for each. Moreover, the control of the means of cooperation may make the leader more than first among equals in the direction of the collective enterprise.

The clearest example of this hegemonic irony is perhaps the mechanism of the gold exchange standard, in the stage at which the reserve center effectively frees itself of obligation to convert

[10]Richard N. Cooper, "Prolegomena to the Choice of an International Monetary System," *International Organization,* vol. 29, no. 1, 1975.

[11]Gabriel Kolko, *The Politics of War,* Vintage, New York, 1969, and David P. Calleo & Benjamin Rowland, *American and World Political Economy,* University of Indiana Press, Bloomington, Ind., 1973.

its liabilities into gold or other reserve assets. This mechanism then allows the reserve center to fight a war without paying the bill—as Britain did to the extent that Egypt and India accumulated sterling balances during World War II or as the United States did through the accumulation of dollar balances in the hands of unwilling holders after 1965, when some part of the dollar outflow was attributable to the Vietnam War.

Moreover, both perspectives tend to confuse three related but distinguishable concepts—cooperative leadership, hegemony, and imperialism—and they fail to distinguish objectives from means. *Cooperative leadership* exists when a sense of common enterprise informs a joint activity, at least in major part. The leader uses persuasion to convince the others that its end is theirs as well and may in addition provide them with side payments ("bribes" or "sweeteners") that have the nature of private benefits. Sweeteners of this kind may be necessary to secure adequate support for the collective enterprise. For the fact that a country shares in the collective benefit will not alone ensure its government's help in producing it; to the extent that a country believes others will provide the necessary support, it may act as a free rider. The need for side payments to induce support for the common enterprise distinguishes a regime characterized by cooperative leadership from a *hegemonic regime*. In this second type of regime, the dominant member controls the trade, financial, or foreign policy of the weaker members in pursuit of its own ends. Although side payments may still be employed, the characteristic means of hegemonic influence are coercive threats; in view of the likely divergence in ends, bribes ultimately would be too expensive. *Imperialism*, third, can be seen as a dominant state's control over the weaker states' domestic politics (and hence also their external policies). Such an encroachment on effective sovereignty is achieved through a combination of bribes, threats, and finally, as a necessary backup, force.

The real world of mixed common and competitive endeavors cannot be adequately represented by any one of these theoretical models. Thus United States policy toward Western Europe in the postwar years might most accurately be called hegemonic leadership. This label implies a mix of cooperation and control: economic relations, created by political and economic means, have been mainly cooperative; and political relations, solidified by economic means, have been cooperative-hegemonic. In one respect, this mix of hegemony in the milk of cooperation can be seen as necessary in any cooperative scheme in which one member bears the major cost. Since the objectives of governments differ in other policy areas and there is a tendency toward free riding, the predominant member will seek to avoid giving a blank check to smaller nations in these other policy areas.[12]

America's postwar leadership, however, can also be viewed as a natural continuation of its traditional economic expansionism, culminating in an attempt to create an "American century." The nature of United States planning and programs for the postwar period from 1942 to 1946 supports this interpretation. The United States expected a multipolar world in which it would be exceptionally strong, but faced with rivalries from Russia, Britain, France, and maybe China. During World War II, using the leverage provided by its superior economic resources, the United States laid the basis for the postwar economic order that it favored. Since the United States government saw such discriminatory practices as British Commonwealth preferences and bilateral trade agreements as putting American exporters at an unfair disadvantage, it concentrated on dismantling them. In line with its material interest, the United States at this stage became the ideological standard bearer for free trade, a position that had been vacated by Britain under the assault of its deteriorating economic performance.

Now it was Britain that was foremost in demanding adequate cushioning—in the twin forms of financing and safeguards—before accepting exposure to the rigors of the free-trade order. The postwar economic order was thus established on multilateral free-trade principles, hedged with a rich thicket of exceptions and sweetened by financial credits—at first sparse, but soon to become unprecedentedly large. This financing had the function of a side payment to countries that needed to be persuaded to join in the cooperative endeavor. The final shape of the International

[12]C. Fred Bergsten, *Dilemmas of the Dollar*, New York University Press for the Council on Foreign Relations, New York, 1975.

Monetary Fund, established at Bretton Woods in 1944, reflected both these qualifications of the norm of multilateral interchange, and the American loan to Britain of 1945–1946 was further evidence of the crucial role of the financial sweeteners.

The limited capacity of the United States to determine the international economic order actually in force, even at the peak of American military-economic predominance in the immediate aftermath of World War II, is a striking indication of the extent to which relationships between the United States and other major Western powers at this time fell short of unqualified American hegemony. For the striking fact is that the United States was not able to impose its preferred multilateral trading order on the major trading countries. It was able to set the frame for such an order, as embodied in the major provisions of the IMF and the proposed International Trade Organization (ITO). But these provisions themselves had to be considerably modified, as compared with the original United States proposals, to make them acceptable to other governments. The original United States conception was thus weakened substantially by the resulting allowance made for transitional provisions, for exceptions to nondiscrimination and absence of restrictions, and for the ultimate escape by countries from the disciplines of the international system through exchange adjustment. This watering down of the pure milk of free-trade and free-investment internationalism played its part in the rejection by the U.S. Congress of the ITO. More generally, it made the multilateral regime an objective of principle rather than an operational reality.

This is seen most clearly in the outcome of the one significant attempt to follow through the letter of the international commitments: Britain's acceptance, in the summer of 1947, of its obligation under the Anglo-American Financial Agreement (a bilateral loan agreement supplementing and overriding the obligation under the IMF) to make sterling externally convertible. Britain's move immediately led to a massive drain on its inadequate currency reserves, forcing the suspension of convertibility after six weeks; the attempt was generally and correctly dubbed a fiasco. Moreover, the episode stood as a salutary and prominent warning that early implementation of the multilateral commitment would involve major strains on the European economies. But the significant fact in our context—significant because it is customarily taken for granted—is that the lesson derived from this warning was that the conflict had to be resolved at the expense of the international obligations. Weak as they were, the European countries were still able to give priority to what they saw as their domestic needs, even though their actions involved preserving and in some respects intensifying the bilateralism and the autarkic tendencies that the brunt of United States postwar economic policies was designed to remove. In a fully hegemonic system, it would have been the domestic policies of the European countries that would have borne a much larger share of the adjustment to the imposed international environment—as indeed the policies of peripheral countries in the pre-1914 gold standard had been affected.

The direct approach toward a full multilateral system was abandoned after 1947 by the United States as hegemonic leader, at least as an objective for the next stage of policy. Inspired and prodded by the bait of Marshall aid, the European countries turned instead to regional cooperation. The usual interpretation of this sequence is that the United States made a major readjustment in its international economic policies in deference to overriding political and security objectives.[13]

But this interpretation glosses over the failure of the United States to carry out its earlier multilateral goal. Marshall aid and acceptance of trade liberalization on a regional basis discriminating against United States goods were not *alternatives* to the multilateral objective but practical ways of moving toward that goal. The regional cooperation Marshall called for in 1947 did not aim to create a permanent and institutionalized scheme of regional trade discrimination, but urged a move toward temporary and limited European economic cooperation. He sought minimum exceptions to free trade—in terms of both the extent of

[13]"As American leadership came to accept the Soviet diplomatic-military challenge as the major postwar problem, the United States attitude toward international economic relations underwent a drastic reversal. . . . In contrast to earlier emphases on multilateralism and nondiscrimination, the United States accepted discrimination in the interest of rebuilding the shattered West European economy." (Gilpin, "Transnational Economic Relations," p. 409.)

exceptions allowed and their duration—that would help sustain the recovery of the European economy during the crises of Communist successes and economic collapse in Europe. Thus what the new political-security considerations associated with the perceived Soviet threat provided was an additional incentive for the United States to finance and endure the long road that it seemed was the only approach to implementation of its multilateral economic objectives. Without that incentive, the outcome would much more likely have been bilateralism and autarky, perhaps eventually emerging in regional blocs with no special affinity to the United States rather than anything resembling the IMF-ITO regime. This situation reflected fundamentally both the primacy accorded to domestic objectives, notably to full employment, in the political economy of the time and the partly associated belief held by European countries that independent action was a better means to these objectives than adherence to an international economic order that constricted the level of output and employment by excessive exposure to an unfavorable international environment. This policy contrasted with the external primacy that had been accepted in most economies, at least up to a fairly advanced point of domestic discomfort, until 1931. This is not to deny that the wider security considerations gave the United States its own incentive to avoid unduly abrupt adjustment of the European economies.[14]

According to this interpretation, therefore, the United States—by providing massive additional *financing* and accepting trade and payments liberalization by *stages*—saved rather than abandoned its earlier objective of ultimate multilateralism in 1947–1948. Such a policy was then possible because of the fundamental characteristic of the international political economy of the time: United States leadership on the basis of only qualified hegemony. The strategy, as is well known, was a major success: the moves toward progressive regional liberalization, undertaken by European economies that were strengthened by the aid injections, paved the way for a painless adoption of multilateralism at the end of the 1950s, with the moves to currency convertibility

[14]We are grateful to William Diebold for comments on an earlier draft of this section.

and the ending of trade discrimination against dollar imports. United States finance played a double role in this strategy. It not only increased the strength of the European economies, thereby making moves toward regional and ultimately multilateral liberalization less painful and more attractive. [The United States could not at this time foresee that formation of the European Economic Community (EEC) would give regional discrimination a permanent and less acceptable form.] In addition, and of central interest to this essay, the United States' financial injections provided an integral and perhaps decisive binding for the cooperative effort as a whole.

This was seen most clearly in the context of the Marshall aid program itself, in which European countries received their aid allocations in the context of their cooperative efforts in the Organization for European Economic Cooperation (OEEC). The American connection was also transparent in the European Payments Union, in which the United States made a direct contribution that was available, in effect, to compensate the "losers" from the EPU system of regional convertibility. In effect, in both cases the United States' contributions provided private benefits to countries that participated in the collective effort. These benefits thereby deterred free riding, which is the bane of any collective activity dependent on voluntary support. As an outsider with a money bag, the United States solved the collective good problem in this stage by easing cooperation with side payments.

Yet side payments by themselves were not enough. Reliance on them alone would have exposed the United States not only to a disproportionate share of the costs of military and economic cooperation but also to a loss of control over the use made by other countries of resources acquired through the cooperative enterprise. Therefore to protect itself from these hazards, the United States had to make its political influence dominant. And thus a hegemonic irony lay within the schema of cooperation. The European states were junior partners in control of the joint enterprise; in addition, they lost some control over their national political resources and effective freedom of action in both political and economic policies. In part this loss was the mirror image of the resource gain acquired from the collective arrangements.

Thus the existence of NATO decreased the need for independent national military forces, and the availability of American aid meant that less needed to be invested in national currency reserves. Yet these very benefits reduced the capacity of the European states to take independent action against the wishes of the alliance leader.

Thus the United States was able to apply the hegemone's coercion against Britain and France during the 1956 Suez crisis to force a withdrawal of troops from Egypt. It used both financial and market coercion—most strikingly through its leverage in the International Monetary Fund as well as through its control over Western Hemisphere oil supplies. The United States could justify the exercise of such coercion in collective as well as in national terms, by arguing the need to avoid writing a blank check on NATO defense policies. Yet the hegemonic-cooperative framework of the NATO alliance was to be challenged in the 1960s as the Europeans found their security subject to unilateral changes in strategic doctrine emanating from each new American presidential administration.

In addition to the element of political hegemony in the earlier postwar period, some aspects of hegemonic economic coercion may be seen, more controversially, in certain features within the generally cooperative nature of the economic relationship between the United States and its European partners, e.g., in the opening of the war-devastated European economies to United States investment on terms of national treatment.

The postwar order was created for the First World. The disintegration of the European empires was not envisaged in the wartime planning and was not substantially completed until the early 1960s. United States relations with what was to become the Third World were on the surface conducted on the same basis as relations with developed countries. On the one hand, the European colonies in Africa and Asia were treated as integral parts of the First World metropolis—in effect as domestic problems of Britain, France, or Portugal. On the other hand, the countries of Latin America and elsewhere that were endowed with legal sovereignty were assumed to be developed or readily "developable." The United States based its political relationships on for-

33

mal equality; in their economic transactions, Third World countries were expected to be full participants in the international economy, although helped along with foreign aid. Indeed, both First and Third Worlds were mutually interested in wider markets for certain products. But the greater instability of the political systems of the developing countries and the greater vulnerability of their economies made the impact of the postwar order markedly different for them. The hegemonic component was more salient. The Third World states could be made subject to considerable Western influence as a result of their internal political divisions and because their dependent and fluctuating economies were more likely to come into contact with the enforcement end of the IMF or World Bank. Politically, a lack of national integration encouraged a faction of the elite to sustain itself in power with United States assistance; its consequential dependence on this assistance gave the United States substantial leverage over government policies.

Thus the postwar order reflected in the West a mixture of cooperative leadership on the economic front and hegemonic leadership on the political front. In the Third World, the order appeared to be cooperative but was in fact based on more fundamental structures of hegemony.

SOURCES OF THE CURRENT EROSION

The key problem for any effective international economic order is to build sufficient inducements and/or sanctions as endogenous elements within the system. The ease with which this can be done is dependent in important ways on environmental characteristics of the international system as a whole. From our present-day perspective, it appears that the broadly successful establishment of the post-World War II economic order was based on special, rather than general, supporting conditions.

The changes in relevant environmental characteristics that are in train are discussed below in relation to three sets of influences: (1) the distribution of the relative size of the member countries of the system; (2) the relationship for the various member countries of the perceived benefit from the international order to the sacrifice of potential individual gain from action that runs a risk of weakening or destroying the international order and the consequential extent to which countries' broad interests are linked over a number of issues; and (3) the extent of hegemonic control, particularly vis-à-vis the Third World. All three factors have become less favorable to preservation of an international economic order as a result of politico-economic tendencies that first became evident in the early 1960s and continue in prospect for the 1980s.

Relative Size

Nations that are large in economic and/or political size reap a large absolute benefit from international public goods such as military security or a truce in tariff escalation; thus they can be expected on general grounds to provide more than their *proportionate* share of the costs.[15] The same influences underlay United States support for regional liberalization in the 1950s and the hegemonic aspects of United States leadership in the developed world discussed on pages 25–34. The relative expansion in the European and Japanese economies, which involved an accompanying decline in the relative economic dominance of the United States, has produced a constellation of economic powers that is less favorable to economic cooperation. The decline in the relative size of the United States need not itself have had this effect if it had been balanced by the emergence of a small oligopoly of evenly matched powers, such as the United States, the European Community, and Japan. In principle, a small group such as this one can be expected to be sufficiently aware of mutual interaction that it would thereby provide for the collective good. The problem, as Kindleberger has pointed out, has been that the EEC has not yet acquired the necessary internal cohesion for effective

[15]This theme was first developed by Olson and Zeckhauser in their analysis of NATO's bargaining structure: Mancur Olson and R. Zeckhauser, "An Economic Theory of Alliances," *Review of Economics and Statistics,* 1966.

communal participation in such group leadership.[16] That bargaining and free riding take place within the subgroup itself is reflected in the EEC's eventual position on international economic matters. The most conspicuous facet of this diversity within the EEC is its inability to develop a common external financial policy and specifically to move toward the declared goal of monetary union and a common currency. A more recent indication in the same vein has been the EEC's failure to develop a common energy policy and a common front toward the Organization of Petroleum Exporting Countries (OPEC).

The conflicting interests and positions taken by major EEC countries after the United States suspended convertibility of the dollar in August 1971 were a major factor in preventing establishment of a durable new monetary order. The reduction in the economic and political preponderance of the United States, evident by the mid-1960s, had clearly obviated the possibility that the United States would impose a solution through side payments or sanctions. The market solution of floating exchange rates represented, in effect, agreement to differ. Underlying differences among the EEC states have also inhibited subsequent establishment of effective international rules and procedures on management of floating. Broadly, the lack of a coherent EEC presence in the international financial system has perpetuated the leadership gap in international monetary affairs. Monetary integration within the EEC has often been presented as a way to fill this gap. In practice, the *objective* of monetary integration has done the opposite, inhibiting individual EEC states from playing a more active global role while bringing them no closer to attaining their own regional objective.

The shifts in the size structure of the international economic community have in this way weakened the basis for adherence to an international economic code; no leader, or leadership group in the shape of a cabal of major powers, is available to perform the function of entrepreneur and backstop of the collective good of international cooperation. As a result of this shortcoming, both the large nations themselves and those smaller ones whose ac-

[16]Charles P. Kindleberger, *The World in Depression,* University of California Press, Berkeley, Calif., 1973, pp. 307–308.

tions are influenced by the combination of inducements and sanctions provided by the leadership have less incentive to give primacy to the requirements of the international order over those of their immediate perceived national advantage in specific actions in which the two may conflict. This lack of a leader or leadership group thus diminishes the likelihood of internationally oriented action, even where there is no diminution in individual governments' perceptions of its benefits. The ratio of perceived benefits from publicly (internationally) oriented against privately (nationally) oriented actions may remain the same, yet the incentive for internationally oriented behavior diminishes.

Bipolarity and the Area of Common Benefit

The ratio of public to private benefit in international economic action has itself diminished as a result of global political developments, notably the reduction of the salience of the perceived East-West contest. This situation constitutes a second structural weakening of the basis for an effective world economic order and has had three relevant effects. These involve diminution in common interests, in self-interests to uphold them, and in available sanctions to enforce them. First, individual governments' perceptions of their international interests have increasingly diverged, so that the extent of common international interest (which includes an effective world economic order) has diminished: the public good covers a smaller area and its value is subsequently reduced. Second, to the extent that the reduction in salience of the East-West rivalry involves an absolute reduction in perceived benefits from group action, notably through protection against military attack, there is a diminished incentive to preserve such benefits through other cooperative action. Finally, the diminution of the jointly perceived area of common benefit has reduced the scope for the exercise of substantial influence against members not following the policies of the hegemonic leader.

Specifically, an important indirect sanction on European nations to stay within the international economic code during the period 1948–1962 was their awareness of their ultimate dependence on the United States for security against Soviet attack. Even where the likelihood of attack was perceived to be small, their desire to avoid risk militated against actions in trade or monetary affairs that might jeopardize their security shields. But in the course of the early 1960s, European perceptions of this military security were changed by developments in both military technology and United States policy; the resulting reevaluation differed in important ways for the leading European states. Throughout much of the 1950s, the United States would have been capable of attacking the Soviet Union in a nuclear war without suffering equivalent damage from a Soviet counterattack. This capability was reflected in the strategic doctrine of massive retaliation, which offered the Western Europeans a nuclear guarantee in the event of a conventionally superior Soviet land invasion of their territory. But with the development in the late 1950s of effective Soviet long-range nuclear capability (albeit exaggerated by the West), the United States was prompted by its own interests to reconsider the prudence of a massive-retaliation doctrine. The McNamara doctrine of graduated response (conventional weapons in the first instance, tactical nuclear response next, strategic nuclear response left to a third stage) was the outcome of this reappraisal. For Europe, this new strategy spelled increased security risks in two dimensions. It qualified the automaticity of the United States guarantee; and it increased the potential material and human costs to be borne by Europe, as the initial stages of a defensive war would be fought on its soil, with more European troops and with tactical nuclear weapons. To compound these fears, this drastic strategic reappraisal emerged with little consultation from Washington; NATO was merely to adjust to the new bilateral United States–Soviet relationship.

For Germany, on the front line of NATO defense, little recourse remained but continued strategic dependence on the United States. But Britain may indeed have welcomed the new strategy, as the costs would still be borne mainly across the Channel. Moreover, since the McNamara doctrine more accurately reflected the balance of military forces between the two superpowers, the overall guarantee appeared more credible. In contrast, France was close enough to the battlefield to fear the bombs bursting in air and to incur the need for increased conventional military budgets, yet it was still automatically protected by the NATO front line in Germany. So for France, the new doctrine appeared to have few benefits and too many costs. The doctrine's near-dictatorial emanation from Washington added to its unpopularity in Paris.

It is thus significant that the first major departure from international collaboration on the monetary front—the aggressive gold policy initiated by President de Gaulle in early 1965—was part of a wider design to challenge United States leadership in the Western alliance over the central political and security issues. France's actions in ostentatiously converting dollar balances into gold and in advocating an increase in the official price of gold through the sensational medium of a presidential press conference did not in themselves transgress any formal international obligation. France could, and did, maintain that it was simply adhering to the letter of the Bretton Woods agreement. Nonetheless, its actions violated the spirit of that agreement. Leading economic powers had undertaken a collective approach in the early 1960s to contain the emerging pressures on the international monetary system. That approach consisted essentially in using ad hoc expedients to bolster the existing structure by relieving the United States from the latent excess demands on its gold stock as well as in examining in official international groups the case for at least some more fundamental reform. France, in its 1965 gold policy and again in 1967–1968, indicated its determination to force the pace and preempt the nature of changes in the international monetary order by resorting to unilateral action that departed from the principle of collective discussion and collective responsibility for management of the system. France remained isolated in this tactic at least until the eve of suspension of gold convertibility by the United States in August 1971.

This isolation is revealing because other European countries increasingly shared at least certain aspects of the concerns of the French, notably their growing fears of being maneuvered into a de facto dollar standard. Yet none reflected its concerns in similar action either through the vocal tactic of public statements that would exert market pressure on the dollar or through direct requests to convert dollar balances into gold. This restraint reflected the continuing pull of the United States' nuclear guarantee as well as the need for large dollar holders to consider the effects of their action on United States willingness to keep the gold window open. The fact that France could get away with acting as a free rider on this aspect of the gold-dollar system reduced rather than increased the scope for others to act in a similar way, thus lending what some observers saw to be a paradoxical stability to the gold exchange standard once the system entered the "crisis zone," i.e., once American gold reserves were insufficient to meet outstanding dollar liabilities.[17] The limitation of this diagnosis is that it implicitly assumed that an overriding objective for large dollar holders was to avoid suspending gold convertibility. The more fundamental question was what influences would make this so.

The key country in this context was Germany, by far the largest official holder of excess dollars. Germany was transparently anxious on purely economic grounds to reduce its dollar exposure; in 1964–1965, it succeeded in acquiring additional gold at the expense of the dollar, but in indirect ways that did not involve gold conversion at the U.S. Treasury. When these transactions were highlighted, the Germany authorities strenuously denied their significance in marking a turn away from Germany's policy of avoiding direct pressure on the United States gold stock. Shortly thereafter, in March 1967, the President of the Deutsche Bundesbank, Dr. Karl Blessing, was prevailed upon to write a letter to the Chairman of the Federal Reserve indicating that Germany intended to continue, apparently indefinitely, to avoid increasing the gold content of its reserves at the expense of dollars. The same letter made specific reference to the United States commitments to maintain troops in Germany.[18] The connection between United States costs of supporting troops in Germany and German actions to reduce the balance-of-payments burden on the United States had been established for some time. Its first manifestation was in agreements secured by Robert Anderson, as the

[17]Lawrence H. Officer and Thomas D. Willett, "Reserve-Asset Preferences and the Confidence Problem in the Crisis Zone," *Quarterly Journal of Economics,* vol. LXXXIII (1969), pp. 688–695.

[18]Bergsten, *Dilemmas of the Dollar,* New York University Press for the Council on Foreign Relations, New York, 1975, p. 78.

Eisenhower Administration's outgoing Secretary of the Treasury, for a considerable increase in Germany's direct and indirect contribution to support costs in 1960. The Blessing letter marked a new and potentially far-reaching expansion of Germany's currency commitment, since it amounted to underwriting, as far as Germany was concerned, an inconvertible dollar.[19]

The connection represented the most direct example of linkage between currency policy and "high" foreign policy (i.e., military or diplomatic policy) in this period. Similar linkages can be seen in relationships between the United Kingdom and France on the one hand and their colonial or ex-colonial territories on the other: the metropolitan powers providing defense support and budgetary aid, as well as other special facilities, and the dependent territories holding their reserves in the metropolitan currency. More broadly, the fact that the United States accepted a position as lender and aid provider of last resort, for a period extending well beyond the postwar phase of dollar shortage and reaching deep into the phase in which it was itself dependent on credit support from European countries (witness the Italian loan of 1964 and the British credits of 1964–1965) can be attributed to its broad security considerations. These gave it concern for the economic stability of its military allies and potentially losable nonaligned countries. More recently, United States financial support has been translated into diplomatic support of its policies, e.g., by Britain on Vietnam.

This sort of issue linkage needs to be distinguished from the linkage of different issues in piecemeal actions or transactions, e.g., in bilateral trade deals associated with some quid pro quo in another area of the bilateral relationship. Ad hoc issue linkage of the latter kind has been rightly contrasted by Cooper with trade and currency relationships under the rules of an international order.[20] The broader issue linkage of the former kind, however, may be a crucial support for such an order, as the necessary

[19]On this ground some questions were privately raised within the international official community as to whether the letter involved a breach of the United States obligation under the IMF Articles "freely" to convert official holding of dollars into gold.

[20]Cooper, "Trade Policy."

binding that holds both the leaders and the led to their international commitments. It is, in this sense, the proxy for the private benefits-cum-sanctions that are normally necessary to induce countries to pay sufficient regard to the collective international interest. The criterion for broad issue linkage in this context is that it induces actions that support in some way the functioning of the international economy according to an established set of rules or conventional practices. The significance of this criterion does not rest on the optimality of the resulting order—which may, as did the Bretton Woods system in its final stages, entail decisive drawbacks—but rather in the avoidance of issue linkage on a piecemeal basis that could open the way to a wholesale abandonment of potential collective gains.

"Broad" issue linkage is promoted by (1) the existence of powers whose perceived political and security interests extend over a wide area, so that these powers have an incentive to offer benefits that are valued sufficiently by peripheral countries to induce them to support ancillary aspects of the relationship, including the prevailing international economic order; (2) possession by such powers of a sufficient margin of economic strength to be able to offer such benefits; (3) a high degree of coincidence of political-security interests among member countries of the system, which will increase the perceived value to them of political and economic cooperation and will in that way increase the risks of national actions that threaten the system or their access to it—i.e., free riding will be more hazardous.

The two structural changes discussed above—namely, the decline in the relative economic dominance of the United States and the reduction of the perceived salience of the East-West contest—thus tended to undermine broad issue linkage.

The Decline of Hegemony in the Third World

The compliance of most of the Third World with the postwar politico-economic order was based partly upon the advantages the system appeared to offer to the elites and partly on American economic and political hegemony. In the late 1960s and early 1970s, both the perceived advantages and the hegemony declined.

Economic weakness and instability, coming at a time when expectations in Third World countries had been heightened by political independence, discredited the benefits of international economic integration. These economic difficulties also contributed to the political instability of the Third World regimes. A military technocracy oriented to specifically nationalistic goals came to the fore as repeated military interventions, from both the left and the right, attempted to establish a degree of political order. Typically these new leaders were committed to development and capable of exercising their organizational and coercive capabilities to create the political stability a rapid development program seems to require.

This new internal cohesion, the continuing disillusionment with international economic liberalism, and the decline in cold war ideological solidarity provided the basis and incentive for Third World states to challenge, formally and jointly, the United States–dominated postwar order. The clearest manifestation of this challenge came in the strident meetings of UNCTAD and the Group of 77. But it was not until the Oil Revolution of 1973–1974 that this Third World coalition got a demand for a New International Economic Order on the global agenda. This occurred even though the increase in oil prices worsened the economic position of many of these states, now categorized as a new Fourth World of desperate poverty. The reason was that the Oil Revolution also provided some states of the former Third World, the OPEC nations, with the financial and political resources to lead a challenge to the postwar order which had to be attentively considered by the United States and the Organization for Economic Cooperation and Development (OECD). The UNCTAD coalition stood up to challenge the existing politico-economic hierarchy and the rules upon which that hierarchy was based.

In sum, then, reduced hegemony, reduction in the relative size of the dominant economic powers, and moves away from bipolarity have each tended to weaken the basis of an observed international economic order during the past decade.

DIFFUSION OF CONTROL

The main consequences for international economic relations of the structural changes in the international polity described above are far-reaching. Perhaps the most fundamental effect is that the constitutional basis of the prevailing order has been increasingly questioned as more countries have sought to have their own particular concerns represented. This questioning has been reflected in pressures for wider participation in management of the system, not only in the sense of interpretation of the existing institutional rules but beyond this, in influence over adaptation of these rules to perceived new requirements. The constitution in effect has been open to continuous amendment, and the new rules and interpretations that have emerged have become looser in order to accommodate the reduced tolerance shown by countries for international constraints they perceive as being against their immediate interests.

The failure to establish a coherent and comprehensive substitute for the Bretton Woods order is a prominent manifestation of these tendencies. The proposed new amendments of the IMF Articles, which are now in the process of being ratified, involve nothing less than an abandonment of a specified monetary order. On the central issue of exchange rate practices, the amendments give governments a free hand, in effect, in their choice of regime; they can select a floating rate, a rate pegged to another currency, or a rate pegged to some composite basket of currencies. The international obligation is confined in effect to "good behavior" in implementing whatever regime is chosen, which means that states should avoid competitive depreciation and conform to "firm" guidelines that the IMF is, in principle, to draw up. It remains to be seen whether any advance can be made on the existing informal guidelines, which are so general as to be deprived of practical significance in influencing particular actions. The commitment to good behavior is far from unimportant. It represents a facet of the wider commitment to continued international collaboration. Yet mere commitment to collaborate, without substantive specification of the basis for collaboration, represents a qualitative weakening in the basis of international action.

In form if not in substance, it takes the international monetary order back to the Tripartite Monetary Agreement of 1936. This is not to deny that a regime of nationally managed floating, even under inadequate international surveillance, may still be preferable to the more ordered but overrigid exchange regime of the original IMF Articles. Also, greater reliance on the market for guidance may reduce certain pressures for political intervention. But the unwillingness of governments to accept market disturbances that they believe they can control or offset leaves a continuing potential for political intervention of an ad hoc kind, with no assurance of international consistency.

Still weaker commitments have been undertaken on another major aspect of the international monetary order, namely, the volume and composition of international reserves. Here, too, countries are given a virtually free hand, and although they are enjoined to formulate their individual policies in the light of international considerations, there is virtually no way in which these considerations can be effectively served by unguided action at the individual level.

A second consequence of changes in the international polity has been a diffusion of influence and control in the relevant organs of the international economy. This trend can clearly be seen within the IMF and the World Bank. In certain conspicuous instances in the 1950s, such as the expulsion of Czechoslovakia from the IMF and the leverage exercised over the Suez loan to Britain, this control was harnessed directly to United States foreign policy. The need for the United States to seek support itself through the IMF in 1961 gave the continental European countries the leverage to increase their own management influence, which they successfully did through negotiation of the General Arrangements to Borrow (GAB)[21] and the associated Group of Ten.

This formation of a rich-countries' club in the IMF was itself a provocation to the excluded countries, which included some high-income nonindustrial countries, such as Australia and New

[21]This special facility was not necessary to provisions of the credits to the IMF that it embodied; these could have been arranged under Article VII, without special procedures and voting arrangements.

Zealand. The counterweight emerged with the establishment of UNCTAD in 1964 and the formation of the Group of 77 within it. Unlike the Group of Ten, which was and is essentially a managerial group in which individual countries press their own interests to the point at which a collective agreement is reached, the Group of 77 is essentially a pressure group, designed to influence the decisions of others. Its technique, which has been generally successful, has been to establish a common position. The Group of 77 had some early success in trade matters, notably in establishing the plan for generalized preferences (though its influence was not so great that it could prevent subsequent erosions in the significance of that scheme through the lengthy exceptions lists). The UNCTAD presence was also a positive and probably decisive factor in thwarting the initial inclination of the Group of Ten to exclude developing countries, at least as full partners, in the planned arrangements that were to eventuate in the special drawing rights facility established in 1968–1969. The Group of 77 played a more active role in the international monetary discussions of 1972–1975, having successfully pressed its claim that these negotiations be carried out under the newly established Committee of Twenty. The Committee of Twenty follows the country representation of the IMF Executive Board and has thereby given developing countries almost half the representation and nonindustrial countries as a whole more than half.

Since voting in the IMF and the World Bank is on a weighted basis, the industrial countries have kept their formal control. But undoubtedly there has been a shift of influence. The solidarity of the Group of 77 has generally held vis-à-vis the industrial countries; the oil- and the non-oil-developing countries have established a common front. As a result, the developing countries as a whole were able in 1975–1976 to exercise an unprecedented degree of influence over international economic and political decisions. The clearest reflection of their impact was the United States government's reassessment of its response to the Third World economic challenge and the reversal by Secretary of State Henry A. Kissinger of the earlier negativism he displayed in the United Nations forums that have been the main scene of the challenge. The substantive results were the United States proposal, advanced in 1975, for an enlarged scheme for compensatory financing within the IMF and the supplementary extensions of IMF facilities agreed on at the Jamaica meeting of the Committee of Twenty ministers in January 1976.

The determination by the United States and other industrial countries to avoid an outright rejection of the demands of the 77 at the Nairobi UNCTAD conference in May 1976 reflected the same forces. The members of OPEC indicated, at least for presentational purposes, that their decision on a forthcoming increase in the oil price would be influenced by the response of the industrial countries to the Nairobi demands. Whether substantive results will follow from the acceptance by the industrial countries of a commitment to study proposals for integrated commodity financing, which were the most controversial of these demands, is another matter.

THREE

Necessary Conditions for an International Economic Order

THE WIDENED AGENDA

The main effect thus far of the increased voice of the peripheral countries in the formal bodies of the international economic community has been to widen the agenda. The central objective of the developing countries has been to match their political sovereignty with "economic sovereignty"; hence the demands for greater national control over the major influences on their economic conditions—commodity prices, the activities of foreign investors, the terms on which natural resources are extracted. Yet these demands represent a fundamental analytical confusion between the concepts of sovereignty and autonomy. What is really sought is economic autonomy: influence over the outcome of economic events, as distinct from the formal right and effective power to make decisions aimed at influencing that outcome.[22]

The limited capacity of political sovereignty to ensure

[22]This distinction can be clarified by a hypothetical example. A Third World country has the right to control foreign investment (formal sovereignty), and in the absence of hegemony, it will have the power to exercise that right (effective sovereignty); the restriction may nonetheless not achieve the intended result of making the country less dependent on foreign capital, which may enter on its own terms or not at all (and this is the limitation on the country's autonomy). Thus *formal sovereignty* concerns legal rights. *Effective sovereignty* concerns the practical power to exercise those rights. *Autonomy* concerns the results achieved by their exercise.

economic autonomy is indeed the underlying rationale for international and regional economic cooperation. A limited pooling of political sovereignty can be the most efficient means of enhancing economic autonomy. But where the asymmetry between political sovereignty and economic autonomy is particularly large, as it is for small and undeveloped countries that are integrated into the international system at key points, there is strong pressure for international action to be concentrated on reducing this economic vulnerability. Thus the main demands for increasing the economic autonomy of the developing countries have been increased financial aid, commodity agreements designed to embody not only stabilization but also a permanent transfer of resources to commodity producers, a shift in the balance of power and influence between multinational companies and host countries, and special safeguards for ownership of national resources. The successful action by OPEC in forcing and maintaining a major increase in the oil price and in reversing the subordinate relationship vis-à-vis multinational companies has been seen as a model, albeit a difficult one to follow.

Each of the instrumentalities listed above for increasing economic autonomy of developing countries increases politicization in the sense that it involves deliberate administrative intervention on a continuing operational basis. But to countries whose terms of exchange would be improved by politicization (as compared with those terms under the previously depoliticized market), the process is likely to appear as a legitimate counterweight to economic subordination or inferiority. The point is perhaps most striking in the context of fluctuations in commodity prices. A fully depoliticized process of price setting, involving commodity markets that are free of official intervention, may produce fluctuations sufficiently large as to have a major influence in destroying political regimes of countries that rely on the commodity for a major source of national income. The most prominent example is perhaps the fall of Nkrumah in Ghana in 1966, which followed a drop of almost 50 percent in the London market's cocoa price over the preceding two years. Thus, to the extent that politicization improves and stabilizes a country's economic situation, it is also likely to counter the impact of economic activity on political activity and perhaps also on the political order and thus to reduce economic dependency. The same process of politicization may, however, produce opposite results in the LDCs—particularly those Fourth World states whose economies, already in desperate straits, lack the commodities necessary to benefit from a consciously politicized market.

Governments of industrial countries have for many decades accepted the principle of political intervention vis-à-vis market forces, both domestic and external, in order to protect the political fabric from the impact of severe market fluctuations. The ultimate rejection in the 1930s of the depoliticized regime of the gold standard can be seen as the crucial move in this direction. The developing countries, with their special interests in exporting primary commodities, seek a similar protection via process politicization in the international market. The fact that effective intervention is much more difficult to achieve at the international level, essentially because there is much less control over all the relevant market constituents, greatly limits its efficacy in practice. Yet this practical difficulty does not reduce those governments' beliefs in the necessity to attain an international analogue of domestic economic insulation. The search for instrumentalities to further this objective is likely to intensify in the 1980s and thus is likely to involve an increase in the degree of process politicization in the international economy.

As a result of these tendencies, management of the international economic system has already been extended over a wider range of both countries and issues, while at the same time it has become looser in relation to individual issues. These tendencies have been the counterpart of some diffusion of economic power, both within the developed industrial countries and toward the more advanced developing countries—notably the OPEC states, Brazil, Mexico, and others. This diffusion of economic power has involved an apparent increase in asymmetries in other dimensions of power, notably in the OPEC countries, which have all become considerable financial powers in terms of their reserve holdings; Saudi Arabia, with $25 billion of reserves, is today second only to Germany in this respect and is expected soon to surpass it. But the commodity power and financial power of OPEC countries are clearly not matched by their industrial power. They thereby have a skewed interest in the main features of the international economy.

This asymmetry, which is likely to persist at least in some degree in the 1980s, could have a variety of implications. The simplest, and that most conducive to what appears from one perspective as a moderate international order and from another perspective as a shoring up of the status quo, would be for the countries that have developed significant power in one or two dimensions to be incorporated into the appropriate global management group. Thus it is widely expected that Saudi Arabia will be co-opted into the informal group of five or six powers (the United States, Germany, Japan, France, the United Kingdom, and occasionally Italy) that form the inner council of financial powers within the wider IMF Committee of Twenty and within the parallel structure of the OECD.[23] But piecemeal co-optation of this kind is not likely to be the end of the matter. While the OPEC countries have been cautious and responsible in the management of their now very large reserves, as is indeed in their own direct interest, the very existence of this reserve strength adds to their capacity to exert financial and economic influence in a variety of ways. It makes them a ready source of aid, credit, and investment; substantial sums have already been committed in this way. The results have been seen not only in the form of the direct influence that follows from such transfers but also, and so far perhaps more importantly, in the leverage that this alternative source of finance has provided to developing countries as a whole vis-à-vis the traditional sources of aid and credit in the industrial countries. The solidarity shown at the international level between the oil- and non-oil-developing countries has made this influence particularly significant.

The availability of alternative finance has strengthened the hand of the developing countries in the politics of economic confrontation with the industrial powers. It would be surprising if

[23]One technical manifestation of this development at the time of writing is that Saudi Arabia is about to establish the right to appoint an Executive Director to the IMF under the rule connecting that prerogative to the amount of funds made available to the IMF through bilateral lending.

this tendency did not go further in the 1980s. This prognosis is not dependent on assumptions of extreme forms of action that have sometimes been broached—e.g., for OPEC to invest in stockpiles of other commodities, such as copper, thereby providing a boost to the formation of similar resource-transferring cartels in other commodities. While limited actions of this sort are conceivable, they must be considered unlikely, if only because the OPEC countries are unlikely to expose their funds to the considerable risks that would be involved in investments in commodity stocks manipulated by producer cartels. But considerable leverage must also be expected from more conventional financial transfers, credits, and investments. The disposition of OPEC financial accruals in the past year has already shown a marked tendency toward a lengthening of the maturity of financial claims, together with some diversification of investment into equities and real estate. This tendency must be expected to go further in the 1980s, at least in the important case of Saudi Arabia, simply on grounds of portfolio diversification. Maintenance of purely financial investment on the scale that is envisaged for Saudi Arabian reserves would involve undue exposure to risks of an unanticipated degree of inflation. While the bulk of diversification of assets is likely to remain within the developed world, the OPEC countries must be expected to follow in the footsteps of earlier financial powers in utilizing part of their funds to exert influence and acquire specific favors through transfers to friendly and client countries.

Another aspect of current global economic trends that is likely to affect the international economic order in the 1980s is the diffusion of economic power that is occurring within the major industrial economies. Previously subordinate groups (including not only ethnic minority groups but also organized labor and working women) are increasing their demands for both a larger share of the fruits of economic activity and greater participation in economic decisions at both macro and micro levels. These related tendencies have increased the influence of producer pressure groups and have thereby also increased actual and potential conflict among them. One result has been an increased sensitivity of governments to disturbances from international economic transactions, including not only imports but also the activity of multinational corporations both at home and abroad. The impetus that these increased demands on the major economies have given to inflation has also prompted some restrictions on international transactions; a prominent example was provided by the United States restrictions on exports of soybeans in 1973, at a time of acute sensitivity to rising food prices.

More generally, since the late 1960s the major industrial economies have faced increasing problems both in the macroeconomic area—in the form of a worsening trade-off between inflation and employment—and in particular industrial sectors. These problems, which themselves appear to be related to the increasing difficulty of reconciling conflicting pressures on the economy, have perhaps inevitably increased the sensitivity of governments to disturbances that are proximately caused by international transactions. So far this heightened sensitivity has not caused any general resurgence of protectionism. Given the difficulties caused by the massive oil deficits and the prevailing combinations of high inflation and unemployment in the industrial world, this avoidance of protectionism represents a considerable achievement that would probably have been impossible without floating exchange rates. It was also helped by the deliberate action taken by the collectivity of OECD countries to link the extensions of special financial aid through the new oil-credit facility to commitments undertaken by the borrowing countries not to introduce additional trade restrictions.

At the same time, the increased tendency for governments to intervene in the troubles of particular industries has had an effect similar to that of formal trade restriction in protecting domestic industry against external market competition. Subsidies and other indirect state actions that support industry are among the more important of the nontariff barriers now under consideration in the GATT. It seems unlikely that any clear-cut criteria can be found to deal with the problem. In this sense, increased domestic industrial intervention seems likely to promote at least some retaliatory action by competing countries in the form of countervailing duties or other trade restrictions. While such retaliatory actions should be minimized—for instance, by confining them to cases in which government support is designed as a deliberate attempt to increase exports or reduce imports rather than as part of general support for domestic industry or a domestic region—a wide area of discretion is bound to remain for all. The most promising way to deal with this problem is to establish principles for compensation of foreign producers whose interests are damaged by domestic protective action and to apply such principles to development of a body of case law.

PREREQUISITES OF A CONTROLLED LOOSENING

The international economy in the 1980s is therefore likely to be a considerably looser regime than the international order established on paper (and at least substantially in reality) in the original articles of the IMF and in the provisions of the GATT. The system is likely to be loose in a variety of ways: replete with exceptions on aspects such as the monetary regime, customs unions, free-trade areas and association agreements, and containing special provisions for developing countries and domestic producers facing injury.

The obvious danger in such a regime resides in its potential instability. Some limited loosening is by no means unequivocally undesirable. It can be seen as a rational response to the earlier tendency, which was most manifest in the 1960s, for economic integration to run far ahead of both actual and desired political integration, thereby forcing countries into suboptimal policy choices. *A degree of controlled dis-integration in the world economy is a legitimate objective for the 1980s and may be the most realistic one for a moderate international economic order.* A central normative problem for the international economic order in the years ahead is how to ensure that the dis-integration indeed occurs in a controlled way and does not rather spiral into damaging restrictionism.

The problem therefore is not to minimize politicization in the process sense of political intervention in market outcomes; it is rather to create a framework capable of containing the increased level of such politicization that emerges naturally from the changed balance of forces in both domestic economies and the

55

international system. The function of the loosened international economic order would be to provide such a framework by setting bounds to arbitrary national action and thereby containing the tendencies toward piecemeal unilateral action and bilateral bargaining that may ultimately be detrimental to the interests of all parties concerned.

If a global distributional norm were generally accepted and could be implemented, the efficient solution would still be to make the basic political determination at the constitutional level regarding the basis for transfers necessary to implement that norm, and thereafter to minimize specific political intervention in market transactions. But no such distributional norm can be expected to be achieved in the 1980s. Since detailed political intervention, even where it impedes efficient allocation of production, can serve local distributional goals (e.g., those of OPEC), there is no reason to expect the minimization of process politicization to be an overriding global norm. Rather, during the 1980s some framework, albeit a looser one than the Bretton Woods–GATT system in its original purity, ought to be preserved to capture the benefits of international collaboration for wider markets and efficient flows of labor and capital. But this objective itself requires, both as normative justification and probably also as a means of implementation, that some distributional sweetener be added in order to make the package attractive to countries that might be *either* better off outside the system *or* capable of destroying it in the capacity of free riders and that can be successfully dissuaded from the destructive role.

This objective will not be easy to implement. The fundamental difficulty arises from the previously discussed structural changes in the international system, particularly the diffusion of power among countries and the increased plurality of their interests. What this amounts to is that the conditions that favored the creation of an international economic order after World War II were special conditions related to the particular structure of a bipolar international system rather than general conditions likely to be reestablished in the decade ahead. If there is again to be an effective global economic order, whether in a new shape or a modification of the old one, special attention will have to be given to the lack of leadership of a dominant single power; the organizational problem of mobilizing the collective interest in the more difficult conditions of collective leadership, including the consultative participation of the weak but strident, will be serious.

The most promising basis for attempting this task might be along the following lines. The first step would be to identify the countries that would accept their responsibility for leadership of the system, in the sense not merely of having a special voice in its management but also of recognizing their own special national interests in establishing and maintaining an observed international economic order. One further helpful, though not necessarily decisive, criterion for participation in collective leadership would be an acknowledgment of responsibility to make some contribution toward resource transfers to poorer countries. The set of Group I countries that fulfill these criteria—whether confined to the first two or extended to include the third, distributional criterion—should not be too difficult to establish. The major trading countries, which are all also rich industrial countries, are natural members. The inner core can be seen as the Group of Five—the United States, Germany, Japan, France, and the United Kingdom, sometimes supplemented by Italy and Canada. This group has the advantage of already having an established managerial position in the international economy. The group might be supplemented both by smaller industrial countries as well as by some of the more advanced primary producing countries, which could include in the 1980s not only countries that have long been classified as developed, such as Australia, but perhaps also some of the more successful large developing countries, such as Brazil and the rich oil producers.

These countries would be sufficiently large that they would be aware of the visibility and certain influence of their actions; thus they would not be in a position to free ride on the cooperation of others. This position would give these countries a special incentive to adopt self-restraints agreed on by other members of the leading group. They would have a corresponding incentive to accept, along with other group members, costs of securing adherence to the established order by other members. This is because the perceived gains to each Group I member from the international order, which cannot be taken for granted without the member's own contribution, may be sufficient incentive in itself.

Group II would comprise those states that are not so large as to perceive a direct incentive to share in the general obligations of Group I members but that are sufficiently large to disrupt the system through maverick action of their own. Nonetheless, these countries would have no claim on grounds of underdevelopment or relative poverty to concessional financial assistance or other special incentives (private benefits) to induce them to stay within the rules of the system. Countries that legitimately could make such claims on the basis of underdevelopment or poverty would be the Group III members.

The most difficult problem in this schema, however, is how to handle the "border states" of Group II. Three types of states fit within this category:

First, there are the financially richer and/or more economically advanced Third World countries, such as Brazil, Mexico, and Iran. Their progress in one or more aspects of economic development makes them ineligible for the favored treatment of Group III members, yet the uneven extent of their progress, and their limited economic size, cannot be relied on to give them sufficient direct incentive for general cooperation per se as Group I members.

Second, the states at the "bottom" of the First World whose industries are currently producing the simple industrial goods that the Third World developing states seek to introduce as export engines of their own development. These lagging developed states will thus have an incentive to refuse preferential access to First World markets and perhaps to apply general protection to their own industries. Italy and Britain are currently the obvious candidates.

Third, there are the Communist states of the Second World. Their participation in the world economy is increasing and their absence from collective commitments becomes correspondingly more significant. Specific measures to draw these states into politico-economic cooperation are therefore desirable. The reasons, however, are not related to the potential of these states for political disruption—we can recall no significant instances of the use by Communist economic states of their economic power to disrupt Western markets on political grounds (although particular actions, such as commodity sales, have occasionally caused economic disruption at localized points). The problem is rather the risk that these states may become overweight free riders.

Group III would comprise countries that are both small in economic size and, by a broadly agreed international criterion, deserving of special inducements. Such a criterion has already been established in the categorization of the least developed or low-income countries of the Fourth World, which are given privileged access to cheap loans in the World Bank and now also, to a limited extent, in the International Monetary Fund. These countries have an established claim to international assistance which provides a basis for the legitimization of side payments granted to them as direct incentives to stay within the agreed international order. Legitimization is important because without it, provision of side payments to some countries may merely whet the appetite for similar payoffs to others—specifically those Group II border states described above. (Group I countries would be, by definition, of a sufficient economic size to perceive their own private benefit from adherence to the collective commitments.)

Yet while financial sweeteners can be justified only to Group III countries, other direct incentives are appropriate and necessary inducements for a wider set of countries, including Group II and Group III itself. Such additional direct incentives can take either a positive or a negative form. The positive form—a voice in the management of the system—is unlikely to be of great practical significance for the economically small countries in Group III, even though it might appeal to middle-size economies in Group II by offering a source of political leverage to compensate those willing to bear a share of the burdens. The smallest countries have traditionally placed a disproportionate value on the prospective benefits of universal participation in international management—as they did with the establishment of the IMF's universally representative Council of Twenty—and universal collective management often conflicts with effective management. Yet even a limited constitutionalizing of the international economic order should not neglect to satisfy and thus gain support from demands for wide participation. Since few costs will be borne by these poor countries and since efficiency does require a directorate limited to a small number of Group I states, the actual form of participation should probably be restricted to at the most a minor representation in management and a widespread participation in the investigation and discussion of present problems and pressing goals. In effect, they would be offered an international platform linked to the management of international economic order—a forum in which to express the present formal equality of states and in which to exert pressure on the dominant economic members.

The most practicable form of applying the negative form of direct incentive—sanctions—is to tie them in with the benefits associated with the collective enterprise. Thus both the benefits accruing to all members for fulfilling their general obligations and the special benefits accruing to members eligible for preferential treatment would be conditional on agreed norms of good behavior. It follows that the greater the specific benefits offered in the context of the schema as a whole, the more feasible it will be to police the system. This connection has now assumed much greater significance because the means of direct policing have been weakened by the decline of hegemony and the diffusion of power throughout the global system. *It is therefore no paradox that although the feasible economic order will be looser than that of post-World War II, it will be more rather than less dependent on the provision of specific benefits as an integral part of the schema.*

Three appropriate forms of such benefits would be financial transfer, special access to markets, and "rent" from development of the seabed. The proposal for allocating special drawing rights (SDRs) to developing countries (Groups III and IIa) on a preferential basis ("the link") has been discussed globally for more than a decade and was accepted in principle by all members of the Committee of Twenty but the United States and Germany. There is an underlying rationale in using a collective global instrument, such as the SDR, as a means of implementing a global objective, such as a transfer of resources from richer countries to poorer ones. It seems very likely that allocations of SDRs in the 1980s would have a development link of some kind attached to them. The recent decision to devote a portion of profits from sales of IMF gold at premium market prices to a trust fund in favor of the least developed countries can also be seen as an operational precedent: it is in effect a gold link.[24]

What is far more problematical is whether SDR issues in the 1980s will attain significant size. This prospect has received an important setback in the uncompleted monetary reform that was made final in Jamaica, since the abandonment of effective international influence on expansion of reserves in other forms is likely to leave little scope for SDR allocations; there is, though, a tendency for reserve needs to be filled in other ways, albeit less satisfactory ones.

Since uncontrolled supply of reserves creates the danger of instability, both through possible excess or deficiency of aggregate reserves and through excessive accumulations of reserve currencies and balances in Euromarkets, a strong case can be made on grounds of monetary control for reconsidering at some stage the issue of global reserve regulation. The intellectual case for such regulation has long been rehearsed in academic literature, and it received a fair measure of acceptance in the Committee of Twenty. The crucial block against acceptance of the principle was the unwillingness of individual countries to give up their freedom to determine composition and size of their own reserves. Acceptance of such restraints needs to be seen more clearly as being part of a collective effort to secure a sound international monetary system. A further legitimate collective purpose is to effect a transfer of resources through the link, which is itself dependent on the provision of a sound basis for SDR allocations.

[24]A less encouraging feature of this gold agreement was the insistence of the richer developing countries that gold profits should partly accrue to them. In effect, as Cooper has pointed out, moderately wealthy countries, such as Argentina and Venezuela, refused to relinquish "their" proportionate share of IMF gold for the benefit of such desperately poor countries as Chad and Bangladesh, even though the arrangement would have involved no direct cost to the former. See Richard N. Cooper, "Monetary Reform at Jamaica," in Edward M. Bernstein et al., *Reflections on Jamaica,* Princeton Essays in International Finance, no. 115, April 1976. This episode may be seen as a forewarning of the "Group II" problem.

Achievement of such a basis in the 1980s appears possible. In this context, the potential use of the SDR link as a sweetener to induce countries to observe certain basic codes of the international economic system could be an important additional consideration. The SDR may indeed turn out to play its most important role *not* as a major portion of global reserves, which has been its declared objective—though the volume and proportion of other reserves would need to be kept under strict control—but rather as a *distributional* instrument and an associated negative *sanction* (being withheld from transgressors) for international trade and payment obligations.

Past experience has shown fairly clearly that by far the most effective sanction in the international economy is the ability to withhold loans and credit facilities. The IMF and the World Bank have used this sanction as a means of promoting certain kinds of domestic policies as well as the international obligations stipulated in their own articles. For the 1980s, there is a strong case for switching the emphasis heavily toward international "regime support." This should include respect of obligations in other institutions such as the GATT, for example, on agreed provisions relating to commodity agreements or cartels. International regime support would clearly be a delicate issue. The leverage available to international financial institutions would be used far more appropriately in the 1980s if it were confined to the specifically international purpose of maintaining the international economic order rather than used for the continued schoolmasterly supervision of the details of domestic programs.

In this context, the emphasis in the new Article IV of the IMF on the primacy of countries' underlying economic and financial policies, rather than of their exchange rate policies as such, seems out of key with the needs of a loosened economic order that gives greater leeway to national preferences in domestic policies. The Managing Director of the IMF has interpreted the new provision as entailing an increase in the attention that the IMF will pay to its members' domestic policies.[25] Attempts by the IMF and its

[25] H. Johannes Witteveen, "The Emerging International Monetary System," address to International Monetary Conference in San Francisco, June 17, 1976, reported in *IMF Survey,* June 21, 1976.

major supporting countries to exert creditors' control of this traditional type seem bound to meet extensive resistance. This approach, therefore, is likely to be consistent only with the use of international influence as a lever applied to countries in desperate straits. The desirable approach is rather to use international influence as a catalyst for a cooperative economic order.

The SDR link, as a sweetener-cum-sanction, could be combined with a parallel instrument on the trade side: some improved form of the generalized preference scheme is one obvious example. The facility would be made available to countries that met their general obligations in the trade and payment codes. An approach of this kind would clearly require a considerable strengthening in high level policy cooperation between the IMF and GATT. Generalized preference, in order to meet the demands of certain of the developed countries that might suffer from Third World exports, might be best effected in the context of an international agreement on access and compensation for deprivation of access. Thus Bhagwati has proposed a scheme under which developed countries that restricted imports from developing countries would be liable to offer financial compensation in the form of government aid according to an established scale.[26] Under the terms of Bhagwati's proposal, the governments of the developed countries would have to weigh the priority of avoiding excessive disruption in their own markets and industries against the costs for protection they would have to pay in additional financial aid. International codes on matters of taxation and treatment of foreign investment, including multinationals, could also be more effectively bound by linking adherence to them to access to the international sweetener.

A further potential source of finance for collective purposes is exploitation of the seabed. The World Bank could sell licenses for using these resources and apply the revenue it would thereby accrue to both a Third World development fund and an adjustment fund for those advanced countries experiencing dislocation

[26]J. Bhagwati, "Export Market Disruptions, Compensation, and GATT Reform," in *International Economic Order*, MIT Press, Cambridge, Mass., forthcoming.

as the result of increased importation of Third World manufac-
tured products.

* * * * *

Current discussions of a new or amended international
economic order frequently include the suggestion of the need for
"a new Marshall plan." In the sense that is usually meant, the
analogy is inappropriate. Neither the nature of the problem nor
the current political-security environment is comparable to the
conditions that underlay the United States' financing of European
recovery in 1948–1952. Yet one key aspect of the Marshall Plan
that was emphasized earlier—the provision of direct beneficial
incentives to recipient countries adhering to a collective
purpose—is a useful and relevant precedent for what is likely to
be a prime need of the 1980s.

Whatever the constitution that might emerge, the variety of
interests at stake and the new necessity for collective agreement
are likely to require a complex balancing of proposals on lines
similar to those discussed above, if even a loosened international
economic order is to be achieved. Although the diversity of
interests itself would make such a negotiation difficult, the same
diversity adds to the necessity for a comprehensive multilateral
negotiation in preference to piecemeal and/or bilateral deals. Just
as in the principle of tariff bargaining itself, the scope of mutual
agreement increases as the range of bargaining is widened.

Yet the difficulty of negotiating a comprehensive international
economic order is obvious. For many countries, the specific
benefits may appear small and will rarely be quantitatively significant in relation to development needs. Yet if the feasible
benefits would be modest, so, in a loosened order, would be the
obligations. The history of existing international economic institutions has shown that countries will endure considerable pain
before cutting themselves off from specific benefits. Perhaps a
bigger practical obstacle to the sort of schema we have proposed
will be the reluctance of the major powers, above all the United
States, to limit their own freedom of action. They may prefer to
exercise what dominance they can rather than undertake the trials
of collective leadership monitored by universal participation.

Political Choice and Alternative Monetary Regimes

Edward L. Morse

Introduction

The task of developing a coherent structure, or regime, within which international economic transactions can provide satisfactory benefits to all parties will remain a political priority throughout the next decade.[1] Although most governments will remain committed to this global endeavor, they will be either unwilling to abide by a full and explicit system of rules or they will seek such different systems of rules that no consensus on the desirable rules or conditions of the international economic order is likely to emerge. This lack of consensus stems in part from governmental misunderstandings concerning the political requisites—and effects—of alternative modes of structuring the international economy. This essay attempts to summarize the major alterna-

[1] A *regime* may be defined in any of a large number of ways. In most discussions, regimes are regarded as highly structured and formally institutionalized mechanisms of governance or political order. Thus they are defined as having the formal features of governments: regularized decision-making structures and rules, executive and regulatory features, mechanisms for aggregating and compromising interests and objectives, compliance norms and mechanisms, and procedures for the settlement of disputes. I am employing a looser definition in this context, since I am interested in nonformalized arrangements. Thus I will refer to Cooper's definition of a *monetary regime* "as any particular set of rules or conventions governing monetary and financial relations between countries." ("Prolegomena to the Choice of an International Monetary System," *International Organization* 29:1 (Winter 1975), p. 64.) Regimes can thus be highly centralized or decentralized, stable or unstable, exclusive or inclusive, and capable of maximizing the goals of their members, all to varying degrees.

tives likely to emerge from this lack of consensus as a means of clarifying the political choices that governments will face in the development of monetary and more general economic structures in the years ahead.

There is no agreement among those professionally concerned with this issue as to whether the lack of consensus is itself a major problem. Fred Hirsch and Michael W. Doyle argue in their essay in this volume that disagreement on what they call the constitutional basis of the international economic order is likely to lead to an increase in the politicization of monetary and other economic relations. With no clear rules governing the proper conduct of foreign economic policy, there will be an ever-growing temptation for governments to take unilateral actions—for "damage limitation" or national advantage—that would increase political friction and minimize the political, economic, and welfare gains for all societies that would otherwise result from a properly functioning economic order. At best this lack of rules would lead to political frictions; at worst it could create a climate of nationalism in which force might once again be used overtly and frequently to arbitrate disputes.

Others are much more optimistic about current trends. They emphasize the degree to which governments—especially in the industrialized West—have been able to cooperate in the face of heightened political obstacles in recent years. Richard N. Cooper, for example, applauds the trend toward "cooperative incrementalism" on monetary issues. He argues that the Jamaica monetary agreement of January 1976 formalized a new de facto regime of flexible exchange rates:

Improvements in global economic management remain high on the agenda of needed international discussion, ranging from stabilization of aggregate demand and control of inflation to management of the oceans. But a basic framework has now been established for the international monetary system, and this represents a major step forward from where we were three years ago. The numerous vital details that remain to be worked out will most likely be done now in the light of work-a-day experience rather than through further efforts in constitution writing.[2]

[2]Richard N. Cooper, "International Monetary Reform after Three Years," *Trialogue*, vol. 10 (Spring 1976), p. 3.

The constitutional approach put forward by Hirsch and Doyle certainly embodies a comprehensive political program of action by which today's central economic powers can defuse frictions among themselves and induce or co-opt others—the "new rich" oil exporters and governments of the LDCs at various levels of economic development—into a more harmonious network of economic relationships. It represents a more coherent proposal than many earlier designs for a world central bank or some other type of specific constitutional order, most of which failed to link the monetary system to the larger framework of international politics.[3]

While the more pragmatic and incremental approach that Cooper recommends is optimistic about the prospects for defusing international economic relations, it avoids specifying rules of conduct for individual governments. Often the reluctance to specify such rules is explained as resulting from the plethora of unknown factors that will affect the monetary order. The mechanisms of a flexible-rate system require time to work out. It remains to be seen whether European efforts to create a common monetary policy will succeed and, if they do, whether the shape of the international economic order will be radically different from what it would be if they fail. Also, the effects of the increases in oil prices on who has monetary power and responsibilities will require years to sort themselves out.

Neither approach seems to me wholly satisfactory. The constitutional approach puts forward a specific and interrelated set of prescriptions for avoiding what it sees to be disorderly consequences of pragmatism; it fails, however, to review the benefits and liabilities of alternative constitutional orders and assumes that economic processes can be separated from the substance of political disputes. The "pragmatic" approach stops short of a confrontation with the actual choices that are likely to govern the eventual paths of the monetary order's probable evolution; its proponents believe that such an analysis is either impossible or

[3]This is as true of Keynes' bancor proposal at Bretton Woods (J. M. Keynes, *Proposals for an International Clearing Union*, Cmd. 6473, HM50, London, 1943) as it is of Robert Triffin's various evolutionary schemes (e.g., *Our International Monetary System: Yesterday, Today and Tomorrow*, Random House, New York, 1968.

unnecessary.[4] Yet in many respects, a review of alternative regimes that might eventually characterize the monetary system is both possible and potentially useful. It is possible because the political constraints and incentives that are likely to impel or impede government choice in the evolution of the monetary system can, in large measure, be mapped out, even if we cannot predict specific courses of action that individual governments may take. Moreover, an outline of alternative regimes that might characterize the monetary system can potentially be useful to governments. Even if all consequences of one or another regime cannot be discerned, enough can be perceived to provide guidelines (albeit in quite general terms) concerning policies and tendencies to be avoided and goals that are worth pursuing.

This essay is an effort to outline several alternative arrangements that eventually might govern the international monetary system. Like the essay by Hirsch and Doyle, it assumes that continued politicization of international economic relations poses potentially dangerous difficulties for global economic well-being and is thus undesirable. As well, it argues that a pluralistic and tiered international order in which the major Western economies assume central responsibility for the governance of the monetary order is preferable to the principal alternative arrangements. But the analysis embodied in this essay is far more political in orientation. Indeed, the essay begins with an analysis of geopolitical factors that will govern the evolution of the monetary regime during the next 10 to 15 years—but it is not optimistic about the paths that major governments are likely to follow. This analysis is followed by an examination of why resurrection of a "liberal" monetary system similar to the Bretton Woods system—in the sense of a monetary system that can provide a politically "neutral" mechanism, instrumental to other governmental goals—will be difficult, if not impossible. In brief, I will argue that the emerging monetary order will be "global" in some respects for the first time ever, but that decisions by individual governments will be primarily defensive and oriented toward domestic problems.

[4]There are, however, a number of efforts at describing the parameters of choice. See in particular Cooper's pioneering essay, "Prolegomena," pp. 63–98.

Such a monetary order could take any of a number of forms: it could be a highly centralized regime, a system (like the one proposed by Hirsch and Doyle) based on co-management by the Western industrialized states, one based on regional monetary areas, or a highly fragmented order resulting from a reassertion of narrowly defined national interests. After an analysis of these possible arrangements, the essay will conclude with a brief statement concerning why I think a tiered system based on management and rule application by the member countries of the Organization of Economic Cooperation and Development (OECD) with participation of less developed countries in rule making is the most desirable alternative.[5]

---

[5]The Organization for Economic Cooperation and Development, located in Paris, was founded in 1961 and evolved from the Organization for European Economic Cooperation, which was the European organization set up to help implement the Marshall Plan. The OECD's 24 members include inter alia the United States, Japan, Canada, and all the members of the European Common Market. Hence, the OECD is often used as a shorthand to describe the advanced industrialized West, although some of the members are neutrals or are only somewhat industrialized. (See Miriam Camps, *"First World" Relationships: The Role of the OECD,* the Atlantic Institute for International Affairs and the Council on Foreign Relations, Inc., Paris and New York, 1976.)

ONE

Geopolitical Choices and International Monetary Regimes

Two general factors are central to the delineation of alternative monetary regimes: first, the trend toward international market integration, as it serves paradoxically both to enhance and to restrict in different ways the attainment of specific goals of national policy; second, the trend toward greater national assertiveness in efforts to buffer national economies from increased interdependence or from the declining ability of governments to achieve a growing number of goals of national policy. The tension between the integration of global financial markets and the fragmentation of the major political units that belong to the current international monetary system—and how this tension is resolved—will largely determine the parameters of alternative monetary regimes.

International market integration among the advanced industrialized societies is perhaps the most significant trend to emerge in the international economy. Following World War II, trade among OECD countries grew at the astonishing annual rate of nearly 8 percent, an unprecedented level of direct investment among these economies developed, and the Eurodollar market (with its extension to places like Singapore and Nassau) expanded. The effects constituted a stress on the Bretton Woods system that was unforeseen by its founders and partly responsible for its demise. Market integration is scarcely likely to decline; quite to the contrary, it is likely to increase in the decade ahead. Financial markets are also likely to change in form in the following ways:

- Increased and more symmetrical flows of capital among the Western industrialized, market-based nations, including direct investment in the United States
- Growth in the use of Eurodollar markets by the governments of less developed countries for the purposes of financing trade and development projects
- Greater access by socialist-bloc governments to Western capital markets for financing trade and investments
- Increased use of international financial markets by OPEC governments, both for foreign investment purposes and for financing trade and domestic investment

The upshot is clear: *As never before, certain aspects of the international monetary system will involve virtually all the societies of the world.* The global character of this monetary system will require new forms of regulation and management. Yet international control will be difficult to achieve[6] if only because a widened net of international controls would involve governments and national regimes of such diversity in structure and objectives that international consensus would be increasingly

---

[6]Although this is not an appropriate place to argue the extent to which interdependence brings about such losses in control or even to catalog the types of losses involved, the following quotation from Richard N. Cooper provides a useful summary: "Most national economic policies rely for their effectiveness on the separation of markets. This is true of monetary policy, of income taxation, of regulatory policies, and of redistributive policies (whether the last be through differential taxation or through direct transfers). Increased economic interdependence, by joining national markets, erodes the effectiveness of these policies and hence threatens national autonomy in the determination and pursuit of economic objectives. The term 'threaten' is used nonpejoratively; there are also economic advantages to the joining of markets, and in some—but not all—cases these outweigh the resultant loss of economic autonomy; indeed, that is what creates the predicament. It is aggravated by the fact that during the past few decades the peoples of all industrial countries have substantially raised their expectations of governmental activity in managing the economy with respect to employment, inflation, growth, income distribution, and a host of other objectives, leading to the emergence of what is sometimes called the welfare state." ["Economic Interdependence and Foreign Policy in the Seventies," *World Politics*, vol. XXIV, no. 2 (January 1972), p. 164.]

difficult to achieve. Moreover, no global mechanisms will be able to eliminate the tensions between interdependence and national autonomy. In grappling with these tensions, governments will retain a significant freedom in "managing" the monetary system. They will be able to move in one of two directions: toward greater centralization and internationalization of decision-making procedures and monetary instruments or toward greater reliance upon national autonomy by the adoption of mechanisms to buffer themselves from some of the effects of interdependence.

Regardless of their orientation, Western industrialized societies will continue to play the central role of managing the monetary system. Although some of the current actors may well "drop out" of the managerial club and new ones might enter for selective purpose, the goals of the system will remain essentially those of the historically liberal Western societies: the maintenance of a monetary system that is instrumental to the liberalization of trade. However, these goals will have to be modified, since not all of the governments that will be brought into the management of the monetary order will share historical liberal values; and Western societies will themselves modify their traditional values as they adapt to changing circumstances. The belief that gold is less and less useful as a source of reserves and liquidity, for example, may well have to be revised in light of the need to facilitate growth in trade between the Soviet Union and Western states (assuming, as is likely, that the Soviet government will not allow the ruble to become a convertible currency). Attitudes that favor the separation of the management of the monetary order from other aspects of international relations—security, development, trade, etc.—also will likely have to be altered, especially as some reserve-rich countries, such as Saudi Arabia, and new trading centers, such as Brazil, become more politically prominent and link their participation in the management of the monetary system to other foreign policy goals. In short, although the Western industrialized societies will continue to play a major role in the control of the monetary system, they will have to accommodate conflicting views on how the system should be run. One of the key questions that needs to be confronted, therefore, is: What is the scope for such accommodation? How far can traditional liberal values be modified, as Hirsch and Doyle propose, without the order's breaking down through the injection of inconsistent rules and special cases? Or if the Western governments refuse to accommodate nonliberal values, to what degree can they either limit arrangements for governing the system or impose their own values on the rest of the world?

The major participants in the monetary system will share similar motivations for reform or reorientation of the international monetary system. Depending on the circumstances, however, these motivations will lead to different policy conclusions. The primary motivation of governments will be defensive. Governments will seek to reduce the vulnerability of their economies to external interruptions induced by the openness of their economies to outside activities (e.g., to the deleterious consequence that international financial markets can have on domestic demand management, the spread of short-term cycles of recession or inflation, etc.). This would lead them either to reduce their interdependence with others or to institutionalize it via direct international management. The choice they make will depend on the size and openness of their economies and on noneconomic factors, such as international security concerns, or preferences for regional solutions (especially in the case of Europe). Under most circumstances, the more sensitive an economy, the more likely is a government to seek efforts to institutionalize international management.

A government's decision to reduce its economic interdependence will likely lead to efforts that, in reducing the vulnerability of its economy to outside activities, will also increase the vulnerability of other economies to that state's actions, for reasons to be specified below. The second choice—institutionalizing interdependence—would reduce the overall vulnerability of a group of states to outside activities and increase the vulnerability of insiders to each other through the formation of a wider, but also more closed, economic area. Its effect on outsiders (i.e., increasing their vulnerability to the actions of the collective group) could well be the same as that of the first policy choice.

Even if the choice is international policy coordination, government motivations will be derived largely from domestic political considerations. The politics of international economic relations will be driven by essentially domestic concerns and be geared to alleviating internal rather than global inadequacies. Decisions will reflect governments' desires to enhance their positions in managing domestic economies rather than to bolster their foreign policy positions. Since most Western industrialized societies are likely to preserve democratic governmental forms, the domestic orientation of their policies will stem from electoral politics. This will lead all of them to place greater emphasis upon the goal of full employment, even at the sacrifice of either the efficient allocation of resources at home or abroad or stable prices. It will also lead them to place emphasis on the "well-being" of members of society as perceived in the short-term perspective of electoral politics; thus they may very well sacrifice policies whose political payoffs would not be apparent within electoral cycles. These perceptions may result in decisions that will have the effect of "externalizing" governments' domestic problems: governments may try to induce other nations to take actions that would help their own problems of domestic management, or government policies may serve to "export" such problems as recession, inflation, or the lack of adjustment in balance of payments.

Since the governments of those nondemocratic societies that will also play a major role in the international economy are increasingly dependent for their legitimacy on their ability to satisfy the demands of their citizens, they will share motivations similar to those of the governments in democratic societies. Governments will lose legitimacy if they cannot provide jobs, economic growth and opportunity, and a wide variety of social services. But in nondemocratic societies there will be greater government freedom to sacrifice short-term for long-term goals (e.g., to limit wage increases in order to foster investment).

Motivations for monetary reform will be further affected by some noneconomic factors, such as general security policy, goals pursued vis-à-vis the socialist bloc for political purposes, and goals pursued toward selective members of the developing world. General trends in international politics will also affect the evolution of international economic relations. Recently there has been a debate concerning whether the configuration of power in the international system—who has it and how it is distributed—determines the parameters within which economic interactions develop;[7] or whether the emergence of socioeconomic forces that escape national controls has been so great in recent years that these forces have now assumed a life of their own and will limit the choices that individual governments can make.[8] This debate is essentially not resolvable, but it is clear that the evolution of the international monetary order will tend to parallel the evolution of the structure of international society as a whole. This evolution will involve both greater interdependence and greater pluralism. For instance, given the decline of American economic power since World War II, the United States is not likely to reassert its predominance in the management of the monetary order. The system's management will, in short, reflect the growth of a more pluralistic world order. Whether this pluralism will develop in a context in which the industrialized West will agree to preserve a universal framework, or whether it will develop in a context of regional blocs, will be determined by wider issues that lie outside the strict calculation of economic rationality.

In summary, inherent in the present evolution of the international monetary system are several trends, many of which counterbalance each other. The basic dilemma posed for governments in making choices about the monetary order is that of preserving the economic and political benefits of international interdependence while minimizing costs to national autonomy. This dilemma is compounded by the growing pluralism in international society. How the monetary system evolves, therefore, will depend upon how successful governments are in institutionalizing and regulating international interdependence and in creating a regulatory structure in which a set of more or less equal partners

[7]For a sophisticated version of this position, see Stephen D. Krasner, "State Power and the Structure of International Trade," *World Politics,* vol. XXVIII, no. 3 (April 1973), pp. 317–347.

[8]For a series of essays that tend to support this view, see Robert O. Keohane and Joseph S. Nye, Jr. (eds.), *Transnational Relations and World Politics,* Harvard University Press, Cambridge, Mass., 1972.

"co-manage" a system that until now has been "managed" by a predominant party, the United States.

Before examining plausible paths of evolution in the monetary system, it should be useful to review the normative approach that has tended to dominate Western perspectives on how the international monetary order should operate. If the new monetary order is likely to reflect an accommodation to traditional Western liberal values, it is important first to analyze what these values are.

TWO

The "Instrumental" Nature of Monetary Regimes

The Bretton Woods monetary regime—like all monetary regimes—was fundamentally *instrumental* in nature and did not represent an end in itself. It was established largely in order to provide mechanisms appropriate for the achievement of a range of goals. These goals included achieving orderly balance-of-payments adjustment, providing adequate liquidity to finance international trade, facilitating private investments and other payments abroad, stabilizing financial markets and limiting speculative flows, maximizing the effectiveness of national monetary and fiscal policies, and minimizing the harmful effects of inconsistencies both in policies pursued by a single government and in the aggregate of policies pursued by all governments.

Liberals have argued that, all other things being equal, monetary regimes should be judged in terms of their ability to facilitate the achievement of these goals. This argument, of course, poses dilemmas. If liberal goals are inevitably to be compromised as non-Western governments are drawn into the management of the international economy, instrumental mechanisms will become more controversial. This is the implication of the Hirsch-Doyle proposal to depoliticize the monetary arena. Yet in the absence of international agreement on the ultimate goals to be served by the monetary regime—and as an inevitable result of pragmatism and the co-optation of non-Western co-managers—monetary mechanisms will be subjected to increased political manipulation. But, paradoxically, if at some time the instrumental mechanisms become proximate objectives, there might well be room for international agreement on the nature of a monetary regime. That is, if governments cannot agree upon ultimate ends but can agree on mechanisms to facilitate order in monetary relations, they might well be able to construct a new system. Before examining this possibility, however, we should summarize the basic tenets of the traditional liberal perspective on the monetary order. As Cooper has argued,

It is the liberal Western tradition to place as the ultimate objective the well-being of individual members of society (rather than the power of the state, the wealth of the ruling aristocracy, etc.). Individual well-being has both an economic dimension, taken in its broadest terms, and a security dimension, also taken in its broadest terms. The first involves the economic capacity of an individual to pursue his own aims, and the second involves his liberty to do so without unnecessary interference from the state or from other individuals.

At this high level of generalization, there is little dispute between major participating countries over objectives of the international monetary system or over any other set of conventions governing relations among nations or men. Disputes, rather, arise over the best way to obtain these objectives, over means rather than over ends. It is nonetheless useful to state the ultimate objectives from time to time, for it frequently happens that means become proximate ends, and in the pursuit of these proximate or intermediate objectives in ever greater technical detail, actors may lose sight of the ultimate objectives and even compromise them for the sake of achieving some instrumental objective.[9]

An ideal liberal international monetary regime would be designed to defuse domestic political problems associated with adjustment, to facilitate the growth of international trade, and to remove a targeted balance of payments as an objective in and of itself (while at the same time promoting an overall, long-term balance). Such a regime should therefore be as neutral as possible with respect to the ability of some societies to gain advantages—resulting either from the process of adjustment or from trade

[9]Cooper, "Prolegomena," p. 68.

arrangements—at the perceived expense of others. As Harry Johnson has argued,

It may be taken as axiomatic among scientific economists, though not necessarily among "political economists," that the purpose of the international monetary system is to promote as far as possible freedom of competition internationally among both goods and factors of different national origins; and further that to the extent that international monetary arrangements entail permission or necessity to resort to intervention in international trade and payments "for balance-of-payments reasons" they are failing in their primary purpose.[10]

This idealized view of the international monetary system stems largely from lessons drawn from the consequences of both neo-mercantilist trade policies that were pursued in the 1930s and the breakdown of the sterling-gold exchange standard. If a central goal of the international economic order under construction after World War II was the maximization of free competition and the elimination of trade restrictions, that of the monetary system was the provision of some means of achieving this goal—especially by facilitating currency convertibility, providing the wherewithal for national economies to overcome short-term financial disturbances, and establishing an international mechanism for regulating changes in parities. In short, the monetary system was conceived as subordinate to and supportive of the trading system. However, it is no longer perceived as having so limited a role.

The liberal goals noted by Cooper which comprise the ultimate objectives to be served by a monetary system are now clearly open to dispute and modification. An increasing number of government participants in the monetary system do not accept the traditional Western goals of liberalism. To the degree that command economies become integrated into the world economic system over the next decade, these liberal ends will have to be modified. The growth in "socialist" orientations of governments in less developed societies will detract further from these liberal

[10]"General Principles for World Monetary Reform," in Hugh Corbet and Robert Jackson (eds.), *In Search of a New World Economic Order,* Croom Helm, London, 1974; and Wiley, New York, 1974, pp. 160–161.

ends as these societies are tied more closely into the monetary system. Finally, these ends will also be modified as a result of changes within Western liberal regimes themselves: the growth in the domestic pursuit of collective ends in the modern welfare state, as will be argued below, has added a number of nonliberal goals to the ones Cooper has cited and thus inevitably will continue to reduce the priority that will be placed on the objectives of classical liberalism.

Postwar history demonstrates, then, that a neutral monetary system has been exceedingly difficult to achieve, not least of all because some governments felt that they could not gain as much as others from a freely competitive international economy. Moreover, impediments to the attainment of that goal can be expected to increase over the coming decade. Whether these impediments should lead to questioning of the desirability of such an instrumentality is an open question. More certain are the general factors that have undermined its viability, which include the following:

1. *The growth in the interdependence of international markets*. Paradoxically, just as attempts to institute a "neutral" system for managing the international economy helped to create market interdependence, so, too, has interdependence helped to undermine the system's viability. Both trade and monetary rules in the postwar period have been informed by the assumption that one government's foreign economic policies were the legitimate concern of other governments. Thus postwar trade rules were marked by "reciprocity," the universalization of the principle of the most-favored-nation, and the movement toward liberalization. Similarly, in monetary affairs, governments believed that the definition of a national currency's parity and the ability of individual economies to weather short-term imbalances should be multilateralized. Thus the postwar international economy was based on government recognition of international interdependence in terms of the consequences of one government's foreign economic policy upon other economies.

The continued growth in financial integration and economic interdependence in the absence of political coordination served to undermine the system that was designed to manage it. The instruments of government policy that were intended to handle the more ambitious postwar objectives of government policy have often been neutralized by the growth in international capital mobility. The Bretton Woods agreement specifically omitted mechanisms for the management of private international financial markets. Indeed, the fixed-rate Bretton Woods system, consistent with the goal of preserving domestic national economic autonomy, provided for national controls over international capital movements. Once the norm of freeing such capital flows became widely accepted, the fixed-rate system had perverse effects on national economic autonomy; a new instrument, flexibility, was sought to achieve it.

The growth of parallel markets—especially the Eurodollar market—as a fundamentally international aspect of the monetary system also created a new and unanticipated element in the international arena, by serving as a transmission belt linking domestic economic activities in one economy to those in other economies and thus increasing the sensitivity of domestic economic conditions to external factors. The implication is that unlike the Bretton Woods system, a new system will require recognition that one government's domestic economic policies are the legitimate concerns of other governments.

2. *The uses of the dollar.* In a manner unforeseen at the founding of the Bretton Woods system, one national currency, the dollar, assumed special and multiple international roles: store of value, medium of exchange, reserve asset, agency of market intervention, and source of new liquidity. Since the dollar still remained a national currency, the United States government was confronted with a choice concerning the orientation of its economic policies. On the one hand, the government could have sacrificed some of the domestic uses of control of the money supply and thus could have become less able to achieve its domestic goals while maintaining the effectiveness of the international roles of the dollar; on the other hand, the government could have placed greater emphasis on domestic goals and sacrificed some of the dollar's international roles.[11] The choice was never easy

[11]Many people would argue that there is in fact no necessary trade-off between the domestic and international roles of the dollar and that "good" domestic management will be reflected in good international management. Thus mismanagement of the economy during the period when the United States gov-

insofar as this set of domestic-international trade-offs was far more complex than it appears here. For example, those observers who argued that the international roles of the dollar could be best maintained by proper domestic economic management under-estimated the insecurity that the international uses of the dollar created for other national governments that had to rely upon the judgments of United States leadership for control over their domestic money supply. Moreover, the sheer size of foreign dollar assets beyond Washington's managerial reach also under-mined the ability of the United States government to manage the dollar either domestically or internationally, even if it had been able to shift its concerns wholly in one or the other direction. While this is not the place to summarize the debate concerning distortions imposed on the international economic order by the international uses of the dollar, it is clear that the growth in the dollar's role not only severely constrained the ability of the Unit-ed States government to manage the system but also reflected an underlying contradiction in that role.

3. *The increased burdens imposed by governments on mone-tary instruments*. These burdens also made it difficult for govern-ments to maintain a neutral international monetary mechanism. This growth occurred in the realms of both foreign and domestic policy.

In foreign policy areas—which are often difficult to separate from the domestic arena—the monetary mechanisms did not sim-ply have a passive role in defusing the politicization of adjustment or in assuring growth in competitiveness in the international mar-ket. But even if they had been restricted to these purposes, there would have been difficulties: adjustment had become a sticky political issue, not only because parity changes became especially

---

ernment in effect financed the Vietnam War through deficit spending and infla-tion had as a side effect the erosion of the dollar's value. Had the war been "properly" financed, no such erosion would have been necessary. I regard this issue as partially semantic and partially the result of a discrepancy betw en what makes good economic sense and good politics. What matters is that domestic politics in the United States created a trade-off between domestic management of the American economy and United States role in the inter-national political and economic systems.

charged before 1971 but also because adjustment was hampered by other government policies designed to meet other national goals (e.g., full employment and the maintenance for overriding national purposes of industries with declining comparative advantage); moreover, market competitiveness was undermined by the growth in trade in goods and services that, to one degree or another, were associated with enterprises that were exempted from the rules of an ideal market system (e.g., agriculture, enterprises holding monopolistic positions in areas of high technology, and some nationalized industries).

Additionally, however, monetary mechanisms grew to have other uses that either were or seemed to be redistributive and undermined their ability to fulfill the more neutral regulatory roles that they were predominantly designed to play. The provision of additional liquidity to bolster first sterling and then the dollar appeared to have this redistributive role by providing gains to Britain and the United States "at the expense" of others. These gains included not only the provision of liquidity that would be drawn upon exclusively by those two nations but also the freedom from "disciplines" imposed upon other governments that could not repay external debts in their own currency. More recently, plans to link the creation of new liquidity to economic development also had redistributive aspects insofar as they would have provided credits to less developed countries which were not made available to others.

When other uses and burdens of international monetary mechanisms are added to these, it is clear that these burdens overwhelmed the capacity of governments to maintain neutral and more limited uses of monetary instruments. I have in mind such uses as controlling the extensive private financial markets and, especially, integrating the newly rich countries (both OPEC and other financial newcomers) into a managerial club whose members heretofore had been the original industrialized societies.

In domestic areas, too, new burdens were placed on monetary mechanisms. As Johnson argued, "with sufficient international mobility of capital, demand-management boils down to fiscal policy, with monetary policy serving only the function of determining the level and rate of growth of the country's international reserves."[12] But this neutral perspective on the domestic uses of monetary policy is rather unrealistic. However desirable it might seem in some quarters to restrict the uses of monetary instruments in the management of the domestic economy and to subordinate them to fiscal instruments, this view is limited largely to the Anglo-Saxon world.

Monetary instruments have, if anything, gained increasingly widespread use for both short-term demand management and long-term structural planning purposes, especially in Europe and Japan. The money supply is thus manipulated for employment, investment, and counterinflationary-recessionary purposes. Whether or not desirable, this trend is likely to continue. The efficacy of fiscal instruments depends upon national political conditions that do not obtain everywhere, not even in all the industrialized societies. To the degree that they do not obtain, the mix of fiscal and monetary instruments will stress the latter. Fiscal instruments are notoriously weak in France and Italy, for example, except for regressive instruments such as the "value-added" tax. Moreover, the growth in the number and scope of government objectives in domestic matters—whether by reason of increased demands made by politicized publics or because of the need for increased government interventions to manage a highly integrated economy—has led governments to use whatever policy instruments they have available to bolster their domestic managerial capacities. This, too, has led to the multiple and frequently contradictory uses of monetary instruments to assure such objectives as stability of prices, full employment, balance of payments equilibrium, and long-term social and economic changes.

The upshot again is overload on the international monetary regime. The use of national monetary instruments for an increasing number of domestic purposes impedes the maintenance of international monetary rules to facilitate international commerce or ease balance-of-payments adjustments. In fact, it reinforces a movement toward a "new economic nationalism" in the indus-

[12]"General Principles for World Monetary Reform," p. 162.

trialized world which itself is an additional element contributing to the declining consensus on the underlying principles of the international monetary system.

4. *Changes in economic nationalism*. A final set of factors that has undermined the viability of neutral instrumental principles for an international monetary regime is associated with new forms of economic nationalism. This nationalism is "new" in the sense that it results less from the desire to increase national power at the expense of other societies than did earlier forms of nationalism. Its motivations are far more complex, but its effects are similar. Like those earlier forms of economic nationalism, the new one arises from doubts about the desirability or feasibility of a liberal system of world trade based on free-market conditions. The increased reliance on national economic policies challenges the instrumental values the international monetary system is supposed to preserve. It sours the instrumental principle all the more in that governments wish to take advantage of international monetary mechanisms as additional means to help them fulfill goals that are nationalistic in nature and that reinforce neo-mercantilist policies (i.e., those policies a government follows which will benefit it at the expense of—or more than—others).

Several factors contribute to this reemphasis of the national economic framework and are worth examining in that they represent a trend that is likely to continue over the next decade or so. One, which seems to be paramount, stems from the political consequences of the growth in international interdependence. The increased sensitivity of interdependent economies represents a loss of control by governments over their economies. The growth in interdependence increases the number of factors that affect both the short- and long-range goals that governments pursue. This is another way of saying that interdependence serves to reduce the number of policy instruments available to achieve different national objectives. Consequently, the new economic nationalism results from attempts by governments to create new policy instruments that are designed either to achieve positive goals or, as is more often the case, to reduce the vulnerability of domestic economies to activities originating abroad. In this sense, the emphasis on national tools aims less to achieve external policy goals, less to attain international economic power, and more to buffer against imported crises, imported inflation or recession, and consequent loss of control. It is thus a reactive rather than a purposive form of economic nationalism; it stems from an effort to reassert the effectiveness of national policy instruments. Needless to say, its effects can be the same as those of a more positive economic nationalism: namely, exported crises, exported inflation or recession, and exported vulnerability and undermining of control.

There are additional complications that occur in relations among "welfare states." Here, as Jacques Pelkmans has argued:

Autonomy constitutes the basis for the political responsibility (especially of democratically elected political leaders), tied up with the guarantee of /the possibility of/ a considerable degree of discretionary spending. A substantial reduction of policy-autonomy is a threat to the welfare-state; it touches upon the assumed capacity to pursue policies, that is to sustain the fundamental commitment to voters. The lack of control over the outcome of market processes brings them to the mercy of international economic developments and this is precisely what welfare-states do not wish.[13]

Welfare-state governments will thus be propelled simultaneously to increase market and policy interdependence with others and also to reduce both market and policy interdependence with them in order to restrict the consequences for governmental control over the domestic economy. This tension between autonomy and interdependence knows no easy resolution. At times governments follow an impulse to withdraw from international interdependence. At other times governments try to institutionalize policy interdependence with others as a means of controlling their external environments, if other factors support such openness. This is especially the case when they are dealing with such problems as taxation and the coordination of common domestic demand-management policies. Another course of action exists: the common limitation of autonomy by all welfare states. "The

[13] *The Process of Economic Nationalism*, Tilburg University Press, Tilburg, The Netherlands, 1975, pp. 50–51.

loyalty to cooperate is negative: welfare-states 'buy-off' some of the 'beggar-thy-neighbor' policies while leaving sufficient discretion, loopholes and escape-clauses to have the Conventions or Treaties accepted at home."[14] These choices will be treated more extensively below. For the moment it is important to note that one of the continuing tendencies of welfare states—which in today's world implies all advanced industrialized states—is to maintain control over their domestic environments.

Another closely related factor stems from new domestic goals being pursued in the Western liberal states, in part because of the growth in demand by citizens and in part because of the tendency of bureaucracies to expand their domains of decision. These goals relate to equity in the distribution of income, greater economic security for deprived persons—poor, sick, and old—universal education, etc.

As Theodore Geiger argues, "Western societies, for the sake of democratic social-welfare values, have been reversing at a gradually accelerating pace the liberal state's earlier substitution of efficiency criteria for the aristocratic social values of the patrimonial order."[15]

Some societies have been able to manage this substitution of welfare criteria for efficiency criteria through an acceleration of economic productivity; others (e.g., the United Kingdom) have not. This situation is in part responsible for the deterioration in the ability of governments to assure the simultaneous achievement of the "magic square" of policy objectives—stable prices, full employment, balance-of-payments equilibrium, and economic growth. It is also, therefore, responsible for the imposition of government controls that interfere with market forces at the microeconomic and macroeconomic levels domestically and internationally as well. These agents of interference have also frequently carried neo-mercantilist implications. Whether this trend will continue or be reversed in the years ahead remains an open question.

In addition, certain motivations that are more obviously neo-

[14]Ibid., p. 51.
[15]*Looking Ahead,* July 1975, p. 3.

mercantilist in nature and that impede the smooth operation of a "neutral" set of monetary instruments lead governments to control international markets to their own advantage, in spite of the desirability of maintaining free-market conditions in the international system. These motivations include: (1) the pursuit of trade surpluses in order to pay for other foreign policy goals (aid to less developed countries or security commitments including stationing troops abroad, especially in the case of the United States); (2) the efforts to achieve dominance in certain international markets in order to support leading sectors of a domestic economy (computers, nuclear technology, aviation, etc., notably in the case of France) so that a government can maintain control over its own destiny; and (3) the fostering of exports primarily to maintain conditions of full employment and to avoid other, perhaps more politically costly, modes of doing so or to buoy a currency's rate of exchange. Finally, the imposition of governmental standards and other regulations that arise continually from either the pressures applied by domestic interest groups or the tendencies of modern bureaucracies to regulate the internal environment also create neo-mercantilist effects.[16]

Still other factors lead to an emphasis on national as opposed to multinational solutions during a period of generalized recession in the industrialized world. While these factors might not have the same historical force as the factors noted above, under recent conditions they have certainly negated countervailing internationalist forces. The tendency of governments to impose restrictions on imports or capital flows or to subsidize exports in periods of economic difficulty is well known. In the past these measures have been met by countervailing forces in periods of growth or by counterpressures from interest groups not hurt by a cyclical fluctuation. Should the economic crisis of the mid-1970s be pro-

[16]For more detailed discussions of the origins of neo-mercantilistic policies, see Harald Malmgren, *International Economic Peacekeeping in Phase II*, rev. ed., Quadrangle, New York, 1972, chaps. 1 and 2; Ernest H. Preeg, *Economic Blocs and U.S. Foreign Policy*, National Planning Association, Washington, D.C., 1974, chap. 10; and Hans O. Schmitt, "The International Monetary System: Three Options for Reform," *International Affairs* (London), vol. 50 (1974), pp. 193–210.

longed, the neonationalist forces at work are likely to create additional deterioration in the loose "truce" on both ends and means to be pursued in the international monetary system.

These political and economic issues have, in summary, made it difficult, if not impossible, to assure the maintenance of an international monetary order that is both neutral and instrumental to the achievement of a liberal trading order. These issues define, generally, the ways in which the monetary system has become politicized. They also suggest the boundaries within which a new type of monetary system might be instituted. In the next section, I will turn to an examination of alternative monetary regimes. While in theory the universe from which these regimes were selected is infinite, in practice the range of choice is bounded by those constraints I have already examined and is therefore quite narrow.

THREE

Alternative Monetary Regimes for the 1980s

If we accept the premise that governments should—and are likely to—accept more regulation of their monetary relationships in order to maximize their potential benefits from both market and policy interdependence and at the same time preserve some degree of national control over the management of their domestic economies, four broadly distinguishable regimes can be outlined.

1. A highly centralized regime, based on the principle of "global efficiency" with respect to the growth of free trade, on the minimization of financial market disruptions to national economic management, on the defusing of politics associated with balance-of-payments adjustment, and on the facilitation of economic development. Such a regime has been recommended by many analysts as the only long-range approach to global monetary efficiency and stability. It could be instituted by the advanced market-based societies by a deliberate process of long-term planning or, under some scenarios, could come about in a grave liquidity crisis associated with efforts by oil-exporting countries to draw down their petromoney investments to pay for eventual trade deficits, or it could come into being under any of a number of other crisis scenarios. It would be supported by less developed countries since it would provide mechanisms to assure the fixed exchange rates and credit those nations need to facilitate their development goals. A high degree of centralization might also result from the reinstitution of a fixed-exchange-rate regime.

2. A regime based on narrowly defined national economic in-

terests and characterized by the continued fragmentation of the monetary system, marked by the gradual elimination or delimitation of the dollar's various international roles, the bringing under national controls of the parallel international financial markets, and the desire of most governments to reduce significantly the exposure of their domestic economic goals to external interruptions. Although such a regime would be regarded by many observers as a deterioration of the current interdependent system, it is by no means clear that such a system would necessarily reduce significantly the gains from or the desirability of preserving a system of free trade. In fact, however, such conditions would not likely be deemed desirable by all participants in the system. What is clear is that this regime would be oriented to the preservation of national economic controls and the reduction of current monetary "asymmetries."

3. A regime based on regional, or otherwise limited, monetary areas, each of which would work out its own relations with the other regional monetary areas. The motivation for forming such areas would be mixed. As under the second regime, governments would wish to reduce the vulnerability of their economies to external forces, but they would find it in their interests to associate themselves with certain other governments in order to preserve some of the benefits of openness. These associations would also be regional by virtue of strong political incentives, especially the desirability of assuring an equitable distribution of power throughout the world. The regional associations could in some instances be based on key currencies (e.g., the dollar, ruble, yen) and in other instances on internationally composed assets (e.g., Europa, petromoney).

4. A regime based on efforts by the governments of the industrialized market-based economies collectively to manage their market and policy interdependencies, to preserve their traditional liberal values, and to manage their mutual vulnerabilities. The regime would accept the obstacles to the creation of a fully centralized and global regime at this juncture. It would be characterized by essentially incremental departures from the existing system, but it would make far more explicit the "responsibility" of the major OECD countries for managing the system both on

behalf of other societies and in order to encourage global economic growth and stable expansion of international trade. This is the regime that, for reasons outlined below, I find preferable.

These regimes are not mutually exclusive with respect to either the objectives to be enhanced or the treatment of potential reserve assets, adjustment mechanisms, or desired level of market convertibility.[17] But each is based on a discrete managerial principle. Moreover, each has its roots well within the present international monetary system, which reflects several crosscurrents. The roots of an additional regime can also, of course, be discerned within the present one. This would be an asymmetrical regime that placed the dollar and its multiple uses—vehicle for adjustment, official intervener in private financial markets, accepted reserve asset, source of new liquidity, medium of private exchange, etc.—at the center of the major monetary processes. The managerial requirements of a dollar-based system would place special burdens on one government—the United States. I have omitted separate consideration of this regime partly because its contours are relatively well known (since it, essentially, existed from 1945 to 1971) and have received great—if not undue—attention and partly because I have incorporated many features of this system in the fourth regime, which is outlined below.

It is important to note that these regimes are in many ways artificial constructs that are useful for analytical purposes. In reality, aspects of each of these regimes exist now and are likely to exist in the monetary system that emerges over the next decade or so. The future system, however, will stress certain elements and relationships and minimize others. The regimes outlined here represent purer forms than will any system that is likely to emerge. They thus enable us to review the salient features and likely consequences of each regime in a way that a more complex and realistic portrayal would obscure, and therefore to clarify those choices that do exist.

[17]These are the major categories that Cooper uses to define the monetary regimes outlined in "Prolegomena," pp. 66–67. Since the analysis in this essay is more oriented toward the configuration of power in the international system than is Cooper's analysis, I have focused on a different cluster of categories.

Before examining these regimes, it is important to outline the aspects of each that will be highlighted in this analysis:[18]

1. *Premises* The construction of regimes is based explicitly or implicitly on a view of who or what are the major actors (governments, individuals, etc.), why they behave as they do, what objectives they wish to maximize, and what sorts of situations or relationships they wish to avoid. Whether or not a regime will be feasible or stable will depend to a large degree on how congruent its rules are with the behavioral patterns of its members as well as on how compatible each member's objectives are with those of the others.

2. *Rules* Regimes also embody prescriptions concerning how actors should behave. These prescriptions may or may not be codified, although the more formal the regime, the greater will be the codification of desirable and undesirable behavior.

3. *Institutional Arrangements and Decision Making* A regime embodies a set of arrangements that enable member governments to define their collective interests. Among the more important questions with respect to institutional arrangements are the following: Which governments should belong? How should nonmembers gain access to the managed area? How might nonmembers petition for membership? How might nonmembers who gain the rewards of a collective good—such as reserve assets—be taxed? What voting arrangements (equality, weighted, etc.) would be appropriate? How is "leadership" to be maintained in the system (i.e., formally or informally)?

4. *Relationship to Other Objectives* Almost any system or regime devised to "manage" a specific set of relations is bound to have an effect on issues not directly under its jurisdiction. At times this "spillover" is intentional. (A classic example is the IMF monetary system, which was designed to enhance free trade

[18]I am indebted to my colleague, Catherine Gwin, for suggesting these regime dimensions in a staff paper prepared for the 1980s Project. I am similarly indebted to the discussion of these dimensions in Oran R. Young, *Resource Management at the International Level: The Case of Beringir,* Austin, Texas, 1975. (Mimeographed.)

even though the system itself did not regulate trade relationships.) At other times, it is unintentional, at least for most parties. (E.g., the establishment of a European monetary area would reinforce "Europeanist" goals, including the development of European security arrangements.)

5. *Effectiveness*   The effectiveness of a regime refers to its ability to achieve the goals of the regime. As Oran Young has noted: "[T]he most widely accepted goal of this type is Pareto optimality. Thus, any given regime is to be preferred to another if it makes at least one participant better off without worsening the situation of any participant."[19] Other tests of effectiveness relate to the other categories outlined in this section, including the ability of the regime to assure compliance, to minimize perverse distributional consequences, and to maximize other goals that member—and nonmember—governments pursue.

6. *Distributional Consequences*   One of the very important features of a regime in terms of its stability, but one that is frequently difficult to forecast, is the degree to which it is regarded as fair in producing outcomes for its members. Distributional effects are likely to change: if the gains to one or another member seem to be disproportionately greater than was originally anticipated, other members are likely to try to "renegotiate" the ground rules. Both gains achieved by all parties involved in an arrangement and gains for one or a few (at the expense of or in relation to others) are significant. As Fred Hirsch and Michael Doyle put this point in their essay:

[I]nternational economic transactions can produce *both* joint gains for the two parties concerned and a gain for one party at the expense of the other; and most, though not all, attempts to capture these latter distributional gains will reduce the size of the available joint gain. Since in individual piecemeal transactions, the benefits available to a particular party at the expense of other parties will often exceed any associated fear or a loss from a reduced joint gain, the social optimizing condition requires that restraints on pursuit of distributional gains must be

[19]Young, *Resource Management*, p. 53.

embodied in a constitutional framework or order; they cannot be expected to be adequately applied in piecemeal agreements.[20]

7. *Compliance Mechanisms and Procedures for Dispute Settlement* Apart from procedures for decision making and the aggregation of interests, regimes often have a set of compliance mechanisms, including procedures to settle disputes that arise over the interpretation or infringement of rules. Compliance mechanisms usually require some degree of centralization of power within the regime, but procedures for the settlement of disputes can be worked out in a regime even if power remains decentralized (as, for example, is the case in the European Communities), so long as the members regard the regime as legitimate.

8. *Feasibility* Too often regimes are proposed without a thorough analysis of how they might be implemented. Often, too, the question of feasibility is subsumed under the notion that unless this or that action is undertaken, the social system involved will undergo severe crisis; this argument is then taken as sufficient motivation for the adoption of the regime. Questions of feasibility overlap with many of the factors identified above. Thus the degree to which rules and prescriptions coincide with behavioral patterns is a significant consideration, as is the relationship between the objectives that governments are expected to pursue within the regime and those they pursue independently. A number of obstacles may stand in the way of the regime's implementation. These obstacles might include a lack of harmonization among the goals of different governments and the effects of implementing the regime on a range of tangentially related matters (including the willingness of nonparticipants to have the regime implemented and their leverage over members). An additional consideration that will affect the feasibility of a regime is its likely stability. Some regimes are inherently unstable, in the sense that they carry the seeds of their own destruction by changing the expectations of their members or the distribution of benefits. Moreover, in some cases the goal of stability may be achieved

[20]See above, p. 21.

only at considerable costs to those who desire it. Finally, it should be noted that in most instances feasibility depends upon the willingness of governments to accept changes from the status quo.

REGIME I: AN INTERNATIONAL CENTRAL BANK

Premise The same logic that led to the growth of national central banks has been used to make the case of the establishment of a world central bank. Proponents of this regime argue that the world is moving ineluctably toward a single society and that the first hints of a global system are now evident in the international monetary area. The inability of governments to resolve inconsistencies between their policy objectives—especially those between the imperatives of domestic economic management and the demands of international finance—and the persistence of the major economic centers in making continued growth in international trade a priority will, it is argued, lead them to centralize the creation of reserve assets and other forms of international liquidity. The automatic transfer of international assets to "backward areas" would solve adjustment problems and minimize the need for changes in exchange rates. Eventually the creation of a single international currency would eliminate the exchange rate mechanism completely.

As governments grow progressively dissatisfied with the current floating-rate system, it is further argued, they will see a return to fixed exchange rates as desirable. Contrary to the expectations of their proponents, floating rates seem to require large-scale government interventions via reserves and through international borrowing; they do not create a situation in which international financial markets provide a way to maintain payments balance. Floating does not create conditions for exchange rate stability, but rather those that induce large-scale fluctuations. Moreover, stable, if not fixed, rates will be sought to facilitate economic planning, especially for governments in the less developed world.

Once governments attempted to reinstitute a fixed-exchange-rate regime, they would be confronted with the familiar dilemma of the trade-off between control over domestic policy and preservation of international benefits derived from the operations of an international monetary order. In order to regain effective sovereignty over some domestic economic policy, they would have to give up sovereignty over the creation of international money. They would, in short, move first toward the creation of international credit reserves and eventually to the development of international central banking arrangements that would have some control over the international money supply. This process would require a centralized political framework within which national policies would, in the long run, become harmonized.[21]

Rules A centralized regime would involve, as a first step, the reestablishment of fixed rates of exchange by the major centers of international activity. Reserve-asset creation via world central banking authorities would provide the mechanism—at first rudimentary—of an international lender of last resort that would provide for the maintenance of fixed exchange rates. Maintenance would imply the close surveillance of exchange rates, symmetrical obligations on the part of surplus and deficit countries, international guidance for domestic adjustment, clear rules governing parity charges, and planned creation of new liquidity. If, as is likely, such a regime would seek to maintain full convertibility of currencies, it would also have to provide for centralized supervision of parallel international financial markets.

Gradually, as international money replaced national currencies and the system moved into the use of a single international currency, not only would the exchange rate system be replaced but also agreement on additional rules would be required for the control of the world's money supply. These rules would have to be designed to assure both international cooperation with respect

[21]The major contemporary proponent of this view is Robert Triffin. For a short statement of his argument, see "The International Monetary System of the Year 2000," in Jagdish N. Bhagwati (ed.), *Economics and World Order; From the 1970's to the 1990's,* The Free Press, New York, 1972, pp. 183–198. A more extended analysis may be found in his *Our International Monetary System: Yesterday, Today and Tomorrow,* Random House, New York, 1968.

to harmonization of domestic policies and the performance of other functions of a world central bank. As the former Chairman of the Federal Reserve Board, William McChesney Martin, has argued,

These functions are to make the behavior of the parts compatible with and conducive to the welfare of the whole—by influencing the behavior of individual nations through both moral suasion and the provision of credit, and by creating international money in an amount sufficient to satisfy what would otherwise be the incompatible objectives of individual units with regard to the accumulation of reserves.[22]

The rules would have to be formulated in universal terms. Although initially they would apply only to the adherents of the system and would thus not be global, any government could, if willing, join the new monetary authority and gain its benefits by accepting its rules. But membership would also entail unprecedented international restrictions over national sovereignty, especially with respect to control over the creation and supply of money. But the obligations and responsibilities of advanced industrialized Western countries would likely differ from those of less developed trading partners in the process of industrialization, newly rich oil countries, and socialist-bloc countries.

Institutional Arrangements and Decision Making The only realistic centralized system would be one whose internal structure would be confederal or federal. World central banking arrangements, in short, need not require the establishment of a single world central bank. One of the mistakes made in early efforts to define a world central bank was the fallacy of implying that a single authority, or superbank, run by international civil servants would be required. To be sure, this system would require the enlargement in scope and effectiveness of centralized international institutions, but several "solutions" that fall short of a single superbank are plausible.

Under one proposal advocated by Robert Triffin, regional

[22] *Toward a World Central Bank?*, The Per Jacobsson Foundation, Washington, D.C., 1970, p. 20.

superbanks would be developed[23] and would loosely coordinate their banking functions through either confederal arrangements or an international overseeing agency. These regional superbanks might be similar in structure to the parts of the Federal Reserve System in the United States, but here the "member banks" would be much more autonomous. Another plan, which would be more centralized, would resemble a federal arrangement in which a central authority—perhaps the International Monetary Fund—would be charged with such functions as world reserve creation and would serve as "lender of last resort."

A third possibility is perhaps the most likely. As Martin has argued, world central banking functions are already being carried out by a variety of national and international bodies, including the Federal Reserve Bank of New York, the IMF, the OECD, the Bank for International Settlements (BIS), and the International Bank for Reconstruction and Development (IBRD).[24] Centralization need not involve much more at first than closer governmental coordination of central banking functions through these international institutions. Martin's own proposals in this regard are closer to the reality of the pre-1971 monetary system than they are to today's world. Still, if we assume that there will be efforts to return to a world of fixed exchange rates, proposals similar to his will have to be considered: IMF control over the creation of money through the regulation of the volume of reserves, use of internationally created assets for stabilization purposes, and use of a world central banking authority as a "restraining conscience" over governmental temptations to overexpansion and inflation.

Perhaps the most difficult aspect of decision-making arrangements has to do with "voting" and control. The most realistic proposals for centralization perhaps provide the best solution. If

[23]"The maximum that I would dare hope for, in this respect, is that exchange-rates among regional monetary areas far wider than the present national States will be operationally recognized as a matter of collective interest, calling for collective, rather than unilateral, decisions." (Triffin, "Monetary System," p. 193.)

[24] *Toward a World Central Bank?*, pp. 13–20.

central banking functions are to be carried out by a series of overlapping formal and informal institutional arrangements, then many of the difficulties associated with centralized international organizations could be avoided. The IMF, for example, by continuing to develop as it has in recent years, could combine equal participation of member governments in the discussion of issues with "representative" arrangements (via its enlarged body of Executive Directors) in central decision making. Closer coordination of domestic economic policies, both in the subgroupings of OECD countries and among individual centers of the world economy and their principal trading partners in the less developed world, could reinforce policies formed in the IMF. Even if, however, governments remained the principal actors in managing the international monetary system, much wider latitude would have to be given to international civil servants for carrying out the functions of international monetary creation and regulation via (at least initially) international financial markets and surveillance of national economic adjustment. When, eventually, world money replaced national currencies, nonnationals would have to gain central roles in handling direct transfers within the monetary area. In short, the system would inevitably be a mixed one. But it would have to make more explicit and formal some of the informal arrangements currently embodied by the Group of Ten major monetary countries formed in the early 1960s to create new credit arrangements, or among the Big Five—the United States, Japan, Britain, France, and Germany—which began in the mid-1970s to meet informally to discuss harmonization of economic policies (sometimes supplemented by the participation of Canada and Italy).

Relationship to Other Objectives The system would be oriented to the growth of international trade, the stabilization of international financial markets, and the depoliticization of international adjustment issues. It would also seek to defuse some aspects of the more general politicization of international economic issues—particularly the claims for either redistribution of international wealth or "participation" as a means of increasing national prestige. It would, in short, represent an amalgamation of Western liberal values adapted and modified to a highly interdependent international order. It would try to do this by creating a political framework in the international economic system which would be congruent with the growing integration of international financial markets.

Just as under the other regimes discussed below, one of the principal concerns under a centralized regime would be the management of domestic economies: governments would wisely see that the only way they could preserve effective economic sovereignty in the long run would be by relinquishing it in the short run. If neither flexible exchange rates nor fixed exchange rates in and of themselves can provide for reassertion of economic autonomy, only a centralized international solution would be acceptable. As Triffin argues:

Such a crowning achievement [the adoption of a single circulating—as well as reserve—currency for the world as a whole] should indeed be within reach if the twin goals of exchange freedom and stability, so often affirmed even by the most nationalistic policy makers, were to be taken at face value. The merger of national currencies into a single world currency would, of course, require national sovereign states to accept collectively decided monetary disciplines and to relinquish their "sovereign right" to the use of their national money-printing press. Identical—and indeed stiffer—disciplines and renunciations of sovereignty would, however, be equally entailed in their firm and irrevocable adherence to free and stable exchange rates. The more expansionist countries would be forced, willy nilly, to bring their rate of monetary expansion in line with that of other countries, in order to avoid continued reserve losses that would otherwise make it impossible for them, in the end, to preserve free and stable exchange rates.[25]

In short, the integration of the international economy would force governments to harmonize their domestic policies. Therefore governments would seek out the solution to the adjustment problem which would maximize benefits for all parties: the centralization of the political structure underlying the international economic order. This solution would entail the subordination of

[25]Triffin, "Monetary System," p. 192.

other goals of policy, e.g., those related to East-West or North-South issues, to monetary and trade objectives.

Effectiveness   This regime would serve not only to stabilize international markets, but also to enhance the continued growth in trade. Thus the principal economic goals of the regime would be achieved. However, both the domestic motivations for establishing the regime and the conflicts between objectives pursued within the framework and those pursued independently by member governments would impede the regime's effectiveness.

It is not at all clear that the regime would enable governments in the long run to achieve their "true interests" with respect to adjustment and harmonization of national economic policies. The assertion that it would assumes that far more is known about the way international economic interdependences work than may in fact be the case. Other mechanisms for dealing with loss of economic autonomy—including various regional solutions—might well prove to be much more effective. This might be especially the case if there were reason to doubt that governments would relinquish to international bodies their authority to create money. These authorities would then have to force governments in rich societies to make direct transfers to poorer ones, with the result that governments would lose effective control over those transfers.

The same conclusion might be reached with respect to the relationships between the objectives to be achieved in this regime and other objectives—including foreign policy goals—pursued by governments. It is hard to imagine how this regime could effectively make governments subordinate the latter to the former. Even if a centralized regime could be created in a situation in which governments in crisis decided to create a real international lender of last resort, it is by no means clear that in the longer run the priorities of the moment of crisis could be sustained. Indeed, one could argue that if the regime were created and if the international monetary system were thereby depoliticized, governments would then increase the value they placed on the abilities of nonmonetary instruments to resolve their conflicts of interests with other governments; this unrealistic burden would eventually infuse the monetary system as well, thus tearing it apart. In short, like so many other solutions to international interdependence that concentrate on centralized international institutions, this one assumes the prior existence of—or general and widespread desire for—those characteristics in international society that it is designed to create.

Distributional Consequences As Cooper has argued, several types of distributional issues, including the question of seigniorage—rents gained from use of a national currency—as well as other distributional questions stemming from the use of national currencies as reserves (enhanced freeom for reserve center, prestige, etc.[26]) are raised in discussions of monetary regimes. A centralized regime would certainly help to solve disagreements that arise from use of national currencies as reserves. Gains would clearly be produced for all parties, and the centralized regime would have to embody constraints on the pursuit of individual distributional gains at the expense of joint gains. The argument here is that it is politically more acceptable for all parties to have the seigniorage gains given to the central authority that issued international currency than given to any national governments. While this might be true in the long run, two additional problems are raised in the short run. One has to do with trust. Here again, the regime encounters the difficulties that characterize all centralized solutions to international problems. How can governments be induced to trust international authorities to ensure that distributional gains will not benefit some societies at the expense of (or in relation to) others. The other problem relates to the uneven distributional effects that a world monetary system would entail; namely, that in attempting to depoliticize some distributional issues it would politicize others. For if it is to remain stable, a centralized regime would have to provide for global redistribution in the form of resource transfers from richer to poorer areas. The politicization of distributional issues such as

[26]See his "Prolegomena," pp. 69–73. Since so little is known about the distributional consequences of various types of monetary regimes, I will in all cases restrict my remarks concerning those consequences to issues that I think are clear.

this one already complicates and impedes efforts to create a European monetary union. Why should one expect this distributional issue to be any less severe on a global basis?

Compliance Mechanisms and Procedures for Dispute Settlement[27] Obviously a centralized regime requires to a greater extent than other regimes institutional mechanisms for resolving differences among governments over the regulation of reserves, the creation of money, and the distribution of seigniorage gains. The regime assumes, however, that the incentives of governments to resolve their differences over these and other managerial issues will be high. Paradoxically then, compliance mechanisms can work only when they are least needed and only over technical issues. This does not mean that a centralized regime would require only a minimal amount of dispute-settlement procedures. Quite to the contrary. But the issues that would likely be raised would have to relate to technical problems alone. If fundamental political issues were in question, it is hard to see how any centralized regime could maintain its effectiveness.

Feasibility Although it is difficult to minimize the need for centralized arrangements in the monetary area, it is equally difficult to minimize the obstacles to attaining them. Two major issues should be considered here. First, it is not clear that a regime that moved toward greater centralization could be maintained, given the low likelihood that governments would be willing to live with its consequences. Second, in the short run, it is not clear that governments can sufficiently resolve their differences over what such a regime should look like to be able to agree to its establishment.

Under this latter heading, several problems might be singled out. In addition to national differences over distributional preferences and the problem of trust, Cooper outlines three problems that characterize the selection of monetary regimes and are especially difficult to accommodate satisfactorily under centralized institutional mechanisms: (1) different weighting of priorities by

[27]Here too, very little can be said about compliance mechanisms for all the regimes under consideration. In most instances, therefore, the discussion is brief.

national governments (which might, in fact, facilitate political trade-offs in negotiating centralized arrangements, but would also reduce the effectiveness of the regime's mechanisms); (2) different national preferences with regard to significant problems, including what is to be harmonized (e.g., the willingness of some societies to tolerate higher inflation and others to tolerate higher unemployment); and (3) disputes concerning the relative effectiveness of different arrangements for achieving specific ends, even if governments could agree on those ends.[28]

The problem of trust raises a whole range of fears that currently characterize government attitudes toward centralized solutions and ought not to be minimized: fears on the part of non-Western governments of relinquishing their own values to those of the industrialized, market-based economies that would predominate in any realistic, centralized regime; fears by all governments concerning diminished national control over domestic economic management; fears of loss of domestic and foreign freedom of choice in pursuing policies involving economic instruments; and fears among all governments concerning who would control the new international apparatus. All these fears impose almost insuperable obstacles to the establishment and maintenance of a centralized regime, except in its loosest form. Thus the behavioral premises upon which this regime is based are unrealistic; they do not sufficiently coincide with the regime's necessary rules and prescriptions to make the regime viable.

REGIME II: A FRAGMENTED SYSTEM OF SOVEREIGN NATIONAL ECONOMIES[29]

Premises   Recognition by governments that a fully effective international mechanism, even if desirable, would not be feasible,

[28]"Prolegomena," pp. 74–84.

[29]My analysis of this alternative owes much to Lewis E. Lehrman, "The Creation of International Monetary Order," in *Money and the Coming World Order,* New York University Press for The Lehrman Institute, New York, 1976, pp. 71–117. Yet my depiction of the regime differs in significant respects from Lehrman's, especially with regard to exchange rate regime and uses of gold.

and an exacerbation of loss of control over both the domestic and international economic environments would lead governments to retrench into the national framework of policy action by developing new national instruments at the expense of the maintenance of international institutional arrangements. This could occur either through a deterioration in the will of the developed countries to cooperate or through separate nationalistic reactions to attacks made by governments in the so-called Southern Tier. As under regime I, the major premise of government action would be to decrease national economic vulnerability to activities in other economies and to increase national economic control over the domestic environment. But the means of doing so would be strikingly different because of the assumption that a world of "contained national currencies" is more fully congruent with a fragmented international political order. Elements of the new economic nationalism would thus prevail over other incentives. As a result, in comparison with their functions under regime I, under regime II the kinds of international functions that money and institutional arrangements would play would be significantly downgraded.

Rules A fragmented regime would be one in which governments would seek to maximize their own economic preferences, primarily through national means. National preferences for full employment as opposed to stable prices would inevitably differ, as would preferred trade-offs between short-term stability and long-term growth or between free trade and international financial convertibility. Since there is no single behavioral premise upon which such a regime would be based, it is very difficult to depict a set of rules for it.

Governments would, of necessity, have to be able either to float their currencies freely (the likely mode for major centers of economic activity) or, in the case of smaller open economies, to tie their currencies to those of their primary trading partners. Such actions would result increasingly in retrenchment from the use of any national currency for international purposes.

While such a regime would inevitably be loosely constructed, it need not lead to chaos in the international economy. A new equilibrium exchange rate would likely be reached—but not in the

111

form of fixed rates or even negotiated rates—if only because governments might seek to stabilize their trade relations with one another. They could do this, for example, by negotiating long-term trade contracts involving specified quantities of goods or services at predetermined prices in an increasing range of trading sectors. This does not mean that over the long run such a system need relinquish liberal free-trade goals. Once such a system were instituted, governments might in fact be more able to reinstitute a free-trade regime without fearing financial breakdown than they would be in systems in which one government played a reserve currency role. Indeed, a system of nationally self-contained currencies would theoretically be fully compatible with the emergence of a centralized but constricted means of international payments, albeit retrenched in scope. If floating worked, this system would also be compatible with a large, parallel international financial market. Rules for floating would emerge slowly and flexibly and would stem from experience.

Institutional Arrangements and Decision Making The major institutional requirements of a fragmented regime would be informal. The major centers of economic activity would have to meet to work out, on a de facto basis, the *shalls* and *shall nots* of floating and to share ideas about—and compromise upon—medium-term economic targets. Centralized and formal institutions would play a far more limited role than they would under regime I, but they would still be required and desirable. They would be a repository of the system's "conscience" in the sense that governments participating in informal arrangements would likely want to justify their freedom to act informally by appealing to the "rules" of a more general agreement. Moreover, to the degree that rules governing international financial markets would be required, they would best be established in an international setting in which all those who benefited from and could potentially abuse the operations of those markets could participate. This is likely to be the case for the command economies of the socialist world as well as for the Southern tier countries whose need for access to money markets will be all the greater under this regime. Finally, centralized institutions could also play a research, training, and service role for meeting managerial needs of administrators from the Southern tier.

Relationship to Other Objectives This regime would serve to enhance national economic autonomy, but its effects on other economic objectives, such as trade, price stability, or employment, are indeterminate to the degree that these objectives reflect different priorities of individual governments. In general political terms, the regime would seek to enhance the viability and desirability of national autonomy and international balance rather than free trade, as in the case of the Bretton Woods system. But if the regime worked well, free trade would not suffer. Balance would stem from the recognized values of pluralism in international society and of equality of all governments in assuming rights and obligations. No asymmetries or "financial hegemonies" would be tolerated. No country would be exempt from disciplines or rules of the system, as was the United States in the gold-exchange system. Special rates for key currency countries would be regarded as incompatible with a just international equilibrium. Economic openness, however, would not be regarded as incompatible with equilibrium. A regime based on the new economic nationalism would by no means be autarkic, but would attempt to balance economic nationalism with the benefits of efficiently operating international markets.

Effectiveness Theoretically this system could be compatible with free trade and at least with a recognition that governments have an obligation to respect the sovereign rights of others to enhance their domestic economic goals; yet it is by no means clear that such a system could endure. A system that was based on the validity of national controls for the enhancement of domestic economic objectives would place no clear limitation on the abuse of economic nationalism. Governments armed with an array of new domestic controls would be likely to sacrifice even the core of international interests to which they might initially agree. A climate in which national economic controls are highly valued is also one in which economic nationalism is more likely to be abused. Not only would governments be able to take economic actions that could damage others but, more important, such a system would create an international climate detrimental to international cooperation.

Another direction would of course be possible if it appeared that this regime, like the first one, would carry within it the seeds of its own destruction. Governments could well feel that the uncertainties and loss of secondary and tertiary goals that would result from this system of self-contained national currencies could be reduced through the creation of regionally based—or even wider—arrangements. Such a movement could well be buttressed by governmental desires to curb the domestic sources of neonationalism that would have a perverse effect on governments' abilities to achieve their own economic goals. Governments would then undertake to create new international institutions or to reinforce those rudimentary ones that they would have kept as a means of creating greater certainty and gains that would benefit all parties.

Distributional Consequences One of the principal motivations behind the establishment of this regime would be the elimination of the inequitable distributional consequences of the current regime, which is based on the reserve currency center's achievement of both seigniorage gains and extra freedom at the expense of those who use its currency. The new regime's major feature and goal would be the establishment of an order in which joint gains within the monetary system would not be lopsided. Not simply international balance but also international justice require the elimination of this inequity.

Yet if this elimination represents the chief distributional advantage of the new order, a dilemma is thereby posed: reducing or eliminating lopsided gains in this case involves the reduction of gains from which all parties benefit. For example, the widespread use of the dollar in its multiple roles created extra gains for the United States government, but it also created gains for other parties. The United States government served as a de facto lender of last resort before the demise of the Bretton Woods system in the early 1970s, just as it provided an efficient mechanism for regulating additions to the supply of international liquidity. Moreover, the dollar served as an efficient instrument of exchange and intervention as well as a store of value. Even since the development of a floating-rate system, in which the United States government has ceased to fulfill many of these regulatory functions, the dollar's utility as an efficient medium of exchange and interventionary agent has not declined. To the degree that this new regime would represent a form of national economic encapsulation, many of the joint gains achieved through the uses of the dollar would be lost, with there being no guarantee that the dollar's functions would be replaced through other mechanisms.

Another distributional dilemma is also posed. Elimination of the distributional inequities of the current monetary order will not result in elimination of other distributional inequities related to economic wealth, resources, or productive capacity. Thus, in a sense regime I—the central bank—would be more concerned than this one with the matter of distributional consequences. Under regime II, policy concerns would be focused on buffering far more than on distribution. While the central bank regime would have to be based on active rejection of power imbalances, this one would ironically result in a perpetuation of certain underlying distributional imbalances.

Feasibility[30]   If, as has been argued, regime II would likely be less stable than many of its proponents would expect, it would also confront a number of obstacles that are probably as difficult to overcome as are those of regime I. It should be recalled that the primary motivations for creating this regime relate both to the desirability of buffering a national economy from wholesale deterioration and to the notion that efforts at national encapsulation would be likely further to fragment the international economy. Several obstacles exist that make fragmentation less likely and national encapsulation rather difficult to achieve. In order to implement the regime, private financial markets, which have a built-in strength and quasi-independent status, would have to be brought under control, and current asymmetries based on the dollar would have to be broken down. The technical problems associated with bringing parallel markets under national control or with terminating current asymmetries associated with the multiple uses of the dollar would present major obstacles. The gains to both governments and private banks and corporations from these factors would create countervailing pressures for this regime. Similarly, goals likely to be pursued by major actors, includ-

[30]There are no obvious needs for compliance mechanisms in this regime, whose rules would be largely voluntary. Even dispute-settlement mechanisms could be rudimentary, since whatever rules existed would be worked out largely through political give-and-take among major centers of economic power.

ing the United States, would be incompatible with the conditions of the regime. Why should the United States government, in the name of international justice, be willing to give up processes through which it benefits? Additionally, the creation of this regime would involve a simplification of the "complex interdependencies" that knit societies together across many issues. These complex interdependencies provide benefits that are as valued as would be those of a just international order based on nationally self-contained economies. In short, while governments might move toward creating such a regime, countervailing pressures and goals would limit the degree to which they would find it feasible or desirable.

REGIME III: REGIONAL MONETARY AREAS

Premises   As would regime II, this regime would be based on the recognition that a fully centralized system would not be feasible, although in this case it would also not be desirable. Governments would be motivated primarily by the dual desires to reduce the vulnerability of a national economy to interruptions caused by external factors and to receive the gains from participation in a wider set of arrangements. Under regime III, however, governments would recognize that in a world of societies of unequal size and openness, international balance can be achieved only through the creation of economic areas. Smaller societies would be able to manage interdependence through the optimization of trade within the regional areas, which would remain internally open. The areas would, however, be delimited essentially by geopolitical considerations. In most instances, the members of the monetary area would be geographically contiguous, although it certainly is possible that geographically distant societies might join in the same "region" if they wanted to maintain a high level of transactions for economic or political reasons. Each region would be free to determine its own economic goals, but would balance relations with others through biregional economic agreements, whose rules would result from explicit bargaining processes. These regions might include Europa, dollar, yen, petromoney, and ruble areas. Each region would include both relatively modernized and relatively unmodernized societies, the latter desiring to circumscribe their openness to the global system and to gain secured access to the markets of one or another economic center.

Rules A system of currency areas would have fixed rates of exchange among the members of each area; in some cases the areas might move toward full economic union. Rates of exchange among monetary areas would be determined by free-market forces. The reserve asset, medium of exchange, and source of new liquidity in each area would be either a common international asset (e.g., a Europa) or a national currency (e.g., a yen, dollar, deutsche mark). Private financial markets could be maintained within each region; although regions would differ, some might be centrally, others nationally managed. In any case, financial markets would be limited in size.

Institutional Arrangements and Decision Making Global institutions would be limited in scope to the loose coordination of rules for "managed floating" (as between currency areas) and for settlement of interregional accounts. Within regions a high level of coordination of policy instruments would exist, but the spectrum of regional institutions would be great, ranging from a highly centralized regional system or set of supranational institutions to currency areas run by key national currency states. If the size of interregional trade and investment warranted some change, the scope of interregional institutions could be enhanced by the establishment of a global medium of exchange. But since the primary objective of this regime would be to enhance regional autonomy, the scope of global institutional arrangements would be narrow.

Relationship to Other Objectives International trade and investment objectives would largely be confined geopolitically to the economic area, although there would still be scope for investments across regions by multinational companies. The system would therefore be designed to enhance the economic benefits of interdependence within regions, but to reduce the vulnerability of national and regional economic activity to uncontrolled phenomena external to the area. The system would reduce international market competition across regions within which preferential arrangements would be pursued.

The fragmentation of the world into trade and currency areas would also be pursued for more general foreign policy purposes; economic policy would be subordinated to general foreign policy concerns under the assumption that the most viable and stable world order is one of relatively equal regional centers of power that are each capable of balancing the others, preventing the development of hegemony by any one center, and thereby preserving their own autonomy and identity.

Within each area a bargain would have to be struck between the more developed center and less developed periphery. Fragmentation of the alliance of Third World countries would therefore have to take place, and less developed countries would have to seek out regional bargains for access to the capital, technology, and markets of the more highly developed center. The quid pro quo for the developed countries within each region would be access to markets and sources of supply as well as defusion of political confrontations over economic issues. Sweeteners that they would offer to the LDCs within their regional areas would therefore be likely to have distributional effects, as they do in the global scheme put forward by Hirsch and Doyle, transferring wealth from the rich centers to the poorer periphery.

Effectiveness Regime III ideally would create a stable system of relations among centers of economic power. But its stability would depend on the will and ability of leaders in each regional system to carry out a "rational" balance-of-power policy in dealing with other regional centers. In short, economic balance would depend upon the existence of a political balance in the international system and would reinforce it, at least in the short run. So long as a managed float would work among regions, moreover, no elaborate network of interregional controls over transactions would be required to buffer regions from one another. Whether this buffering by floating would suffice over the longer run would depend on dynamic factors tangential to the monetary domain.

One condition that could make the maintenance of interregional buffering feasible would be the existence of competition among areas for general foreign policy purposes or by reason of a need or desire to externalize domestic social, political, and economic problems. Economic policy, security policy, and other aspects of foreign policy would form a whole and would not fall

118

onto separate "tracks." While proponents of balance-of-power policies would argue that this policy integration would minimize potential conflict between regions, which would coexist in a stable equilibrium, the reverse could just as readily be argued: political and economic instruments could be marshaled for general foreign policy purposes, thus enhancing the potential for reinforcing rather than curbing interregional conflict.

A regional international economy might also be regarded as a way station toward a more centralized regime. In this conception, not only would regionalization be a stepping-stone in the building of international order—rather than an end in itself—but it would also evolve into a more centralized system. Indeed, some proponents of European integration, including Robert Triffin, have taken this view. It is, however, hard to imagine how this could in fact be the case in the absence of some global upheaval. If it could be instituted at all, the regime would likely have a great deal of stability and thus be resistant to any change. If it were not stable, however, it could well move toward a more universal and open international order, as argued in the next section.

Distributional Consequences The distributional consequences of this regime would be mixed and can be summarized on three levels. First, with respect to the international system as a whole, the regime would be designed to create a more or less equitable distribution of power and wealth among the major centers of economic activity. It would thus reinforce the trends toward pluralism and multipolarity of the past decade or so. Its long-term stability would depend upon this interregional distributional equilibrium being maintained, which would require relatively equal gains for all regions or a mild redistribution of power and wealth among regions.

Second, within each regional area distributional issues would arise in the same way as they have within the international monetary area as a whole since World War II. One of these issues is that of seigniorage gains to either individual reserve currency centers or international regional authorities that would become responsible for issuing and regulating regional currency. If the regional authority were to receive the gains, the centralized solution would likely be more feasible in a regional sphere than in the global order of the Bretton Woods system. National reserve currency centers would, however, pose difficult problems since they would likely solidify the regional position of major powers whose political goals other governments in the same area would find suspicious.

Third, an inevitable distributional issue would arise between the more developed industrial regional cores and the peripheral, less developed economies of each region. This is a current issue that is in part responsible for the high level of politicization of the international economy; as in the earlier case, it would probably be easier to create politically acceptable solutions within a regionalized world than it would be in the global context. Direct transfers would have to be made from the richer industrialized societies to the less developed economies, if only as political sweeteners that would make the regional solution more attractive to the Third World members.

The major distributional questions that would arise under a regionalized global economy would thus be microcosmic forms of the issues that confront the international economy today. But industrialized societies within each region would find it easier to grant such transfers, since they would be able to secure tangible political results from them. If sweeteners offered to the less developed members of each economic area were insufficient and fierce competition emerged among the regional centers for markets and sources of supply in other regional spheres, the distributional stakes would then create a fundamental instability in the system as a whole. Under these circumstances, there would be great incentives to nudge the system toward a more global arrangement.

Compliance Mechanisms and Procedures for Dispute Settlement This regime would likely be characterized by a diversity of compliance mechanisms and dispute-settlement procedures within and among regions, ranging from highly developed procedures, as under regime I, to the loosest sort of arrangement for handling disputes arising from interregional arrangements. In the most well-integrated region, where one might anticipate the creation of international currency and a movement toward effective political integration, these arrangements would be similar to those found in federal court systems. The international system as a whole, however, would need to develop nothing more extensive than what might be found under regime II, unless interregional trade and financial arrangements were more extensive than under that regime.

Feasibility   It is not likely that the world economy would evolve into this sort of regional system in the absence of crisis. Indeed, it could be argued that the main motivation for creating this type of system would be the desire to manage interdependence by placing an emphasis on geopolitical controls that would be implemented in conditions of severe and sustained crises in both international and domestic arenas. Under these conditions, such a regime would appear highly attractive to the political leaders of several areas of the world, including those in some of the industrial market-based economies. But in their efforts to create such a system—whether these efforts were inspired by defensive economic and political reactions to crises or by diplomatic design—political leaders would encounter significant obstacles that would be virtually the same as those outlined above under regime II. While this arrangement could create clear benefits—in contrast to regime II—it also would combine the worst aspects of the first and second regimes: it would impose the problems of forced harmony on members of an economic area and the problems of fragmentation on the world at large. Moreover, retreating from the highly centralized and integrated private markets would not be simple; nor would be the effort to reduce "complex, multi issue-area interdependence." Defensive acts to reduce both vulnerability to outside economic pressure and obstacles to domestic economic controls would be contradicted by defensive actions in other diplomatic arenas which might even impede the establishment of regional areas themselves. For example, in security affairs, defensive reactions to external threats might well lead to efforts, especially by Western governments, to bolster current alliance networks. Pressures would thus also exist to prevent regional economic fragmentation along the lines of geopolitical blocs.

In short, the regime could encounter obstacles to its feasibility that would stem from other foreign policy objectives pursued by the major centers of power which cross-cut foreign policy objec-

121

tives leading toward regional constructions. For example, the regime would be contradicted by factors that have bound together the so-called Trilateral areas—Western Europe, North America, and Japan—through direct investments, integrated financial markets, and a highly developed network of trade relations. Finally, it might well encounter efforts by less developed countries to maintain a unified bloc and to push forward on a more global basis political claims against the industrialized world.

REGIME IV: A TIERED SYSTEM[31]

Premises The same pressures that might give rise to the three previously described regimes could also motivate governments of the industrialized world to institutionalize their relations with each other by coordinating their actions so as to reduce the ability of each of them to harm the others and by buffering as far as possible their own network of interactions from outside pressures (i.e., from the less developed countries of the South or the command economies of the East). Governments in the less developed world would want to attach themselves to international institutional arrangements that would preserve a structure of economic stability and order and also guarantee them some participation in the formulation of rules, but they would not participate on an equal basis with the governments of the industrial core.

The motives of the governments of industrialized societies would, of course, be mixed. They would relate in part to the desire to enhance traditional liberal values associated with free competitive markets, but also in part to the desire to enhance the achievement of domestic "well-being" through the closer harmonization of domestic economic policies among the Western industrialized societies. Their motives and goals would create the major norms of the center of the tiered system.

Efforts by these governments to regulate their own economic interdependence through joint management would be coupled

[31]Many of the elements of this system are found in the Hirsch-Doyle essay above in Camps, *"First World" Relationships*.

with other efforts to maintain and reinforce ties with other economies. But since the main motivation for this regime would arise from relations among the market-based Western economies, the effect would be the creation of a tiered system into which other actors in the international economy would integrate themselves differentially without at the same time necessarily accepting fully either the goals or the rules of the essentially liberal Western system. Some efforts at integration would be initiated by the less developed countries; others would be initiated by the advanced nations.

For the economies of the South, special market arrangements would have to be made: a combination of bilateral trade arrangements, special commodity markets (at least to maintain a degree of income stability if not also to involve some level of transfers), efforts to postpone or otherwise relieve debt burdens and at the same time to stabilize private international financial markets, etc. Similar ad hoc arrangements would have to be made for countries of the socialist bloc that wanted to continue to gain access to Western capital, markets, and technology. Similarly, with respect to the Soviet Union, not only would bilateral arrangements with individual Western governments likely continue, but different methods of financing trade—including the use of gold in settling debts—would also have to be experimented with. Finally, informal as well as formal arrangements with all exporting countries would be needed to bring them closer to the central management of the international economy and the international financial network in which they would have special stakes.

The upshot would be a tiered system centered around the five or six Western economies whose international trade and financial levels would continue both to bind them together and to give them a special role. The system would thus be both differentially interdependent and pluralistic and would reflect the messy crosscutting and contradictory factors that are likely to characterize the international economy over the next decade or so. But it would also be ordered. The system would reflect not only the decline of American hegemony or leadership but also the continued predominance of Western economies in a differentially integrating global system.

Rules A tiered system centered around the industrialized economies would have to abandon the traditional liberal norm of universality or at least postpone its applicability until circumstances became more propitious. Since the system would be more or less global in scope and since no single set of rules would either be desirable or acceptable under all circumstances for all parties, different rules would have to be applied to different types of activities and relationships. Yet two overriding and overarching normative principles should be fostered as applicable for the entire international system.

First, any international codes that emerge should embody the notion that what any government does with respect to the exchange rate regime, adjustment mechanism, and mode of handling convertibility is of legitimate concern to other societies. Even a world that is differentially interdependent—with market and financial integration higher among some societies than among others—is a world in which all governments must be concerned with certain of the policies carried out by others. Interdependence is compatible with a pluralistic international order. But it cannot endure, except with perverse effects, in a world in which governments do not recognize that their policies impose unintended as well as intended consequences upon other societies and that efficient management as well as moderation and justice requires that all governments recognize the mutuality of concerns. Second, governments should, as Hirsch and Doyle argue, attempt to implement guidelines for an "economic truce." These would be essentially negative prescriptions that limited the scope of government actions so as to minimize their effects on other societies.

Rules governing the center of a tiered system would of necessity have to be more highly structured and well-developed in some respects. Particularly at the center of the system, means should be found to restrict the degree to which governments are able to manipulate their complex interdependencies. In short, means should be found to restrict the ability of any one of the five or six governments centrally concerned with the financial order to use monetary instruments for noneconomic ends. This is perhaps the most difficult problem confronting the advanced industrialized market-based economies in working out the rules for a new international monetary order.

There will be two main difficulties in formulating these rules. First, it will not be easy to create an apppropriate form of multilateral surveillance to counteract "dirty floating"—the uses of monetary instruments for balance-of-payments purposes and for resisting adjustment. Circumstances will almost inevitably arise, if the exchange rate regime is a floating one, that will lead one or another government to engage in a dirty float. This situation can be avoided only through the abandonment of free floating and the adoption of a principle of relative fixity of exchange rates. Exchange rates would be determined and adjusted periodically—how often would depend upon experience and experimentation—through agreement among the major monetary governments. The center of the system would, in effect, operate along the lines of the Smithsonian agreement of December 1971. Margins of fluctuation could be wide, as they were under the Smithsonian agreement, but parities and ranges of permissible fluctuation would be relatively fixed. Such a system would be the only way to avoid the adverse political tensions induced by dirty floating.

Second, although five or six governments will assume major responsibility for "managing," in the sense of ordering, international financial relationships, they will be able to do so best by a mixture of formal and informal mechanisms. Formal arrangements would govern in the determination of exchange rates and supporting mechanisms. Informal agreements concerning targets for domestic economic goals would permit the development of "common law" in formulating rules to govern an historically unprecedented situation: a high level of interdependence, the lack of a predominant economic power, an emphasis on pluralism, and recognition that what one government does in the management of its domestic economy is of legitimate interest to others. The issue of national sovereignty would be confronted obliquely and informally. Initially governments would create only those formal mechanisms that regularized procedures for the sharing of information on pending government policy actions. Informality would allow for experimentation concerning co-optation of others into the core group for restricted purposes. At times, members of the European Communities which are not in the core group would be co-opted to assure internal European political cohesion; at other times, newly rich oil-exporting states, such as Saudi Arabia or Iran, would be brought in.

To be sure, informality creates envy and suspicion on the part of outsiders which can be assuaged only by making the core group responsible for reporting to a larger and more "legitimate" body in which wider participation of governments is guaranteed. This would be the wider "constitutional order" discussed below. Informality also brings dangers of "ad hoc-ery," as Hirsch and Doyle argue. To avoid this situation, governments within the core should, for their own political purposes, want to be required to report their actions to higher authorities—the OECD at a next and broader tier and the IMF at the broadest—if only to prevent themselves from having to give in to demands made by special interests within their own societies.

The basic rationale behind the standard adopted by the core of the system would stem from a belief shared by these governments that their economic relations with one another have a priority over relations with other societies and that the impact on other societies of their policies is so great that they have a responsibility to coordinate their policy decisions. Policy coordination would also serve as a means of loose global "steering," to use Miriam Camps's term. These rules would involve efforts to stabilize exchange rate relations as noted above, to preserve and to create when necessary common central bank credit facilities, and to maintain financial convertibility through efforts to establish international standards that would preserve parallel international financial markets while limiting their destabilizing effects. These standards should be adopted within a wider framework than the five or six economies at the core of the system itself. At a minimum they should be adopted as a code for the OECD members. A looser code, applicable to others through the IMF, would deal with conditions of access to international credit, whether it is for adjustment purposes, compensatory finance, or a form of direct transfer aid (SDRs). The "inner core" would be open to all those willing to abide by its rules, so that it would be potentially universal.

Once the principle of a multiple-tiered system were accepted, specific arrangements dealing with the access of less developed countries and socialist bloc governments to international credit and participation in "money creation" would need to be embodied in both regional institutional arrangements (which might be part of this regime) and global arrangements (via the IMF-IBRD network). How this might be done is discussed in more detail below. The important point is that overlapping arrangements ought not to be avoided. Rather they should be encouraged because they would reinforce the security of the financial system as a whole and would reflect the complex political and economic linkages among societies. A loosely coordinated global system should have sufficient flexibility to enable governments to accept the rules and responsibilities of whatever particular arrangement is most responsive to their needs. It should also have sufficient flexibility to permit governments to adapt to changing circumstances both by participating in the formulation of whatever new rules become necessary and by moving from one part of the tiered arrangement to another as societies become more developed.

Institutional Arrangements and Decision Making The more highly institutionalized tiered arrangement should be compatible with an IMF of widened scope involving the creation of reserve assets, or credits. The point is that the system would be multi-tiered. The advanced market-based societies would recognize that preserving their own networks of relationships was more important to them than perpetuating other relationships and that it would be irrational for them to expose their relations to pressures from other states. They would thus move away from—but not ignore—global institutions in order to buffer themselves against external political pressures and to ensure that the special conditions of advanced industrialized societies could be preserved.

This does not imply either that less developed countries would be ignored or that they would lose by participating in a multitiered arrangement. The purpose of the advanced industrialized governments' taking actions to buffer themselves against economic and political influences from the South and the East is to maintain the benefits of a liberal order. The advanced nations could argue, pragmatically, that liberal international economic institutions require special arrangements in the evolving international economy. So long as it is clear that the members of the center of the system will not give in to the "demands" of outsiders, others can adhere to their rules if they so desire, but they need not do so.

In a tiered system, the less developed countries would not only participate in the discussion of issues and in the management of certain aspects of information sharing and training for management but would also have a direct voice in credit creation. They would also express their concerns regarding how the central countries co-managed their own network of relations. Two mechanisms would be required. First, the IMF would provide a forum, as it now does in its Board of Governors, for governments to confront issues on the basis of interstate equality: one state, one voice. Second, the Executive Board, which is effectively in permanent session, should be reorganized so that it provides better representation of members; and the principle of rotating representatives, which has so far been avoided in the Fund, should be accepted. This procedure would in effect politicize the Board of Governors; but by making it more representative of the Fund's membership, it would assume that codes adopted for the outer groups would reflect that group's major concerns.

The legitimacy of a tiered institutional arrangement would be satisfied if demands for participation could be met for the outer groups via the adoption of more "democratic" procedures. It would also require that members of the inner core, which would have permanent Governors, would not simply demonstrate their willingness to participate in the wider, more democratic setting but also would react sympathetically to proposals put forward by and in the interests of outer group participants.

Relationship to Other Objectives   This regime would serve to enhance the major objectives associated with the liberal international monetary system: price stability, full employment, free trade, economic growth, and defused adjustment process—goals that, with the exception of free trade, are shared by command economies as well. It would also serve to enhance global economic development, if the major precondition of global development is assumed to be the provision by advanced market-based economies of generally stable conditions in the international economic environment. In this regard, the regime should also embody facilities, such as compensatory finance arrangements, to maintain income stability in international commodity markets—a major concern of the less developed world. The regime would be designed to prevent monetary instruments from being used for the pursuit of nonmonetary objectives; in this sense it would be an effort to keep monetary and trade relations on their separate tracks and apart from the pursuit of other, more general foreign policy objectives.

The objectives of the regime are, however, related to other foreign policy goals. Most important, the regime is designed to be global without being universal. Its pluralistic nature is designed to make the regime as congruent as possible with the overarching structure of political relations in the international system. The regime would not be a pure universal and liberal order; it would be biased at the center toward the values of Western societies and at the periphery to the needs of command economies or economic development. This division of orientations is proper so long as the major participants in the international economy remain Western and so long as others have special needs. This system would not be rigid and could well accommodate the interests of non-Western governments, regardless of their level of development.

Effectiveness   The establishment of this regime would by no means assure complete stability or the total defusing of politics in economic relations. But, as a truce, it would probably go a long way toward enhancing both conditions. If the institutionalized relationship were loose enough to allow an inner club to drop out members whose economic impact on others was reduced over time and to bring in new members when appropriate, it would likely be able to evolve along lines that resembled the more dynamic changes in international economic relations. It would clearly be an "oligarchic" system in the sense that it would single out selected members of the global community as having special responsibility for monetary management. It would contradict a tendency toward interstate egalitarianism in the international sys-

129

tem. This could open it up to potentially destabilizing attack from other governments. But if the Western governments persevered in their efforts to maintain what they consider to be minimal acceptable conditions for enhancing their own values, and if mechanisms were created to meet the special needs of others, the system would likely succeed.

Distributional Consequences   There is no doubt that this regime raises all the distributional issues concerning international financial arrangements which have characterized debates over the reform of the international monetary system for the past decade and a half. The overtly hierarchical nature of the system—which involves efforts both to buy off and to ward off those societies of the less developed world that have most vociferously made distributional claims—will make the system appear as though its distributional effects are lopsided in favor of the Western market-based societies. These distributional effects—or at least perceptions of them—would have to be counterbalanced by what Hirsch and Doyle call "sweeteners" to others. As is argued more fully below, politicization of distributional issues would be defused in the long run if a fully tiered system were accepted. If a tiered system were not accepted in the short run, it does not seem to me that unwillingness by others to go along should impede the effective cooperation of the advanced countries in establishing the core of the system, or the system's first tier.

A major distributional issue would remain, nonetheless. As Hirsch and Doyle argue above, the constitutional aspects of the Bretton Woods framework enabled one government—the United States—to provide a collective good for other members of the monetary order. In the process, the United States government not only had to deal with free riders but also had to "buy off" other members to prevent them from straying from the rules of the system. In return, the United States government gained freedom denied to others to run deficits and collected other seigniorage gains from the use of its currency. The system recommended here would provide for the production of an international collective good that would be consumed by the parties producing it as well as by others. There is no clear set of conditions that have to be met to make this joint production possible and stable. At a minimum, it could be argued that governments will want to manage and curb the perverse effects of interdependence. But the United States will remain a sort of *primus inter pares*. A special difficulty will be encountered, therefore, in preventing the United States from exercising its potential to damage others through unilateral actions and in engaging it to act as a coequal while at the same time exercising some degree of political leadership.

Feasibility[32]   Four major obstacles might be singled out as standing in the way of this regime. First, it could be attacked by nonparticipants who would demand participation in decisions made by others which would have a central impact on their own domestic and foreign policies. To the degree that such participants (either other advanced industralized societies or third parties) could exercise leverage over the members of the club, they might be willing to use "blackmail" in order to ensure the achievement of their own short-term goals. In a world of complex interdependent relationships, it is extremely difficult to prevent governments from manipulating the ties that bind them to others, especially when foreign policy stakes are high.

Second, this regime would depend upon the willingness of the members of the club to work out an economic truce with one another. If the United States or some other government felt that its interest would be served by making policy decisions independently of other members of the club, and if these decisions tended to "harm" others, the viability of the arrangement would be severely reduced. The regime, in short, depends upon the ability of a set of governments to maintain a systemwide frame of reference in managing their domestic economies. This regime also requires a change in perception and orientation by those core governments—especially in Europe—that because they are more

---

[32]There are obvious needs for compliance mechanisms and procedures for dispute settlement in this regime. But they would be as complex and overlapping as the rules required to govern the system. A general outline of how they might be developed can be inferred from the rules and institutional processes of the regime outlined above.

vulnerable than the United States, fear pressures from the less developed world. It assumes as well that differences regarding the structure of the monetary system—which have often in the past, for example, aligned France with some industrializing countries and pitted this alliance against the United States and Germany—can be overcome.

Third, this regime might so impede the achievement of other high-priority foreign policy goals that governments would be unwilling to maintain it. The advanced market-based economies do not form a closed system. The desirability of creating an economic union in Europe or of significantly enhancing economic relations with other societies (command economies or LDCs) might be such that governments would be unwilling to sacrifice those objectives in order to institutionalize an advanced economy network. But as is argued below, these other objectives need not be sacrificed in order to achieve closer cooperation with the United States and Japan.

Fourth, and finally, the regime's success depends in the long run on its acceptability to less developed countries outside the inner club. It therefore depends on the ability of industrializing countries to accept a foreign economic policy different from the ones they have pursued in recent years. If, as seems likely, the industrialized societies remain relatively invulnerable to the less developed countries (even if the latter unite), the LDCs are likely to depend for several more decades on the advanced Western economies for markets, sources of capital, technology, and international stability. The outsiders would likely have little choice but to accept these arrangements, which would, after all, bring them greater benefits than almost any feasible alternative.

Notwithstanding these difficulties and obstacles, there are sufficient incentives and sweeteners to make this regime a feasible and desirable one. Efforts would have to be made to assure governments that their long-term foreign policy options would not be limited by the construction of a relatively fixed international monetary order. This is especially important with respect to the governments of the European Communities that will wish both to maintain their goal of economic union and to guard against their perceived vulnerability to threats to sources of supply in the less developed countries. European union and a managerial club incorporating some members of the European Communities and outsiders (especially Japan and the United States) need not be perceived as mutually exclusive. Indeed, the two might be mutually reinforcing. Moreover, there is no reason to assume that European vulnerability to sources of supply of raw material is nearly as great as some Europeans perceive it to be. European markets, technology, and capital will remain attractive to less developed countries, counterbalancing European vulnerability. The major open questions are whether the market-based advanced nations will have sufficient incentives to constitutionalize their relationships rather than leave them to evolve on an informal basis, and whether non-Western governments will perceive the system to be sufficiently in their interest so that they will cooperate in its development.

FOUR

Conclusions

The regimes outlined above are meant to sketch some of the major directions in which the management of international monetary relationships might evolve over the next decade or so. Since these regimes are composed of clusters of variables, each of which might evolve somewhat differently from the way it is described, a much larger number of clusters and mixtures could have been sketched. Nor need conditions in the "real world" evolve so strikingly in one direction or another as they are outlined above. These regimes are, therefore, not nearly as mutually exclusive as they might appear to be. They represent different hypotheses concerning how and why some of the trends that currently characterize the international monetary order might become dominant under various circumstances.

I have a clear preference for the emergence of a system along the lines of the fourth regime. This preference stems in part from my normative biases toward a more pluralistic international order in which no single society plays such a predominant role that it can abuse the autonomy and freedom of others. As well, it stems from my belief that a clear structure of international order, and preferably one with explicit rules, is required if a durable, just, and moderate international order is to be achieved and maintained and from my belief that the first regime is not feasible. This means that several very difficult problems, some of which were alluded to above, must be overcome.

First, it means that a core group of industrialized Western

governments must independently and collectively assume a "systematic" view with respect to the management of the international economy—and that their collective management must be acceptable to non-Western and nonindustrialized societies alike. It is not important that the views of each of the governments perfectly coincide with those of the others. Rather, what is important is that members of this core group acknowledge that what they do in their relations with one another bears significantly upon what other governments—in the industrialized world outside the core group and in the socialist and less developed worlds—can do. It is perhaps not a pious hope that the growth in interdependence among the Western societies, whose members share a common set of normative attitudes not only toward market arrangements but toward a wider array of questions as well, will continue to bind these societies together economically. If governments realize that the well-being of their own societies is tied closely to that of the others, and that they will, therefore, be unable unilaterally to achieve any of their major goals without inflicting damage upon others, then the necessary binding for tying them together in mutually reinforcing systematic attitudes might emerge.

Second, under regime IV the tasks for American statecraft would be great. What is being requested is that a form of collective leadership be developed in the management of the international economy to replace the individualistic leadership of the United States that has prevailed since World War II.[33] This would require the development of new attitudes within the United States government. The history of American experience with the exercise of international leadership tends to indicate that the United States government either would want its will to prevail (with some limited room for compromise) or would want to withdraw from international collaboration. Yet the specter of withdrawal is not a happy one for most of the rest of the world. Nor is it for the

[33]For good discussions of "leadership" in the international economy, see Charles P. Kindleberger, "Systems of International Economic Organization," in *Money and the Coming World Order,* pp. 15–39; and Miriam Camps, *The Management of Interdependence,* Council on Foreign Relations, Inc., New York, 1974, pp. 96–103.

United States. American withdrawal too often implies disregard for the effects of American actions on others. If collective leadership is to work, the American economic giant must be tamed and the United States government must accept pluralism while it and other participants recognize that as the largest economy in the international economic system, the United States still retains an unrivaled ability to harm others.

Third, the fourth regime will put new pressures on other core group members as well. If the habit of unilateral action is difficult for the American government to break, so too the habit of disavowing leadership is difficult for the Western European and Japanese governments to lose. There is little in recent experience to warrant optimism either that a collective agreement among the European members of the Common Market will lend coherence to international economic relations or that the Western European governments will individually be able to assume a more global perspective concerning the requisites of international economic management. Similar conclusions might be drawn with respect to the Japanese, whose system of governance almost inevitably results in a more introversive than extroversive policy position. More optimistic conclusions might be reached, however, if in stabilizing relations among themselves, the core countries would also provide stable conditions for international economic growth.

Fourth, the problem of leadership and economic management is complicated by any effort at creating a framework of rules within which relationships can evolve. As Kindleberger has argued: "In political terms, the provision of the world public good of economic stability is best provided, if not by a world government, by a system of rules. However, it is difficult to obtain agreement on an adequate system of such rules or the means of enforcing them."[34] A system of rules flexible enough to meet changing circumstances but strong enough to assure the commitment of major governments can, in a way, provide the necessary scope within which the major governments can gain an appropriate freedom of action without at the same time absolving themselves of the responsibilities for the effects of their actions upon

[34]Kindleberger, "International Economic Organization," p. 37.

others. But in such a flexible arrangement, the rules might be too loose to provide the necessary binding.

Fifth, there is the problem of reconciling demands for an egalitarian or democratic international order of states with the inegalitarian distribution of power and wealth in the world. The first issue is often posed as a question of justice; the second as a matter of maintaining efficiency and order. As in so many other instances, the problem is posed as a dilemma, representing a choice between mutually exclusive organizational principles. An international democracy of states, based on the sovereign equality of governments in the international system, is often put forward as the only legitimate means of organizing the international system as a whole as well as its constituent parts. According to this view, the monetary system, like the United Nations, ought to be managed on a one-state, one-vote basis. A more efficient principle of management, which recognized the special responsibilities of the principal participants in the international economy—the rich Western industrialized societies—would clearly contradict the norm of international equality of states. This is not the place thoroughly to analyze this dilemma, but it is essential that these divergent paths be reconciled in the emerging monetary order. I feel that they can be reconciled, if not philosophically, at least to the extent of assuring cooperative behavior and minimizing destructive conflict. A tiered system that recognizes the reality of inequality of economic wealth and power, yet incorporates a wider framework in which any government could participate in the formulation and resolution of issues, is to my mind the only way to assure economic stability and political legitimacy. Smaller countries whose share of international economic activities is minor should want a framework in which they can tie down, regularize, and monitor the behavior of the larger economic powers. And the latter should want to seek out a means of justifying their actions before a wider forum so that a neutral economic environment can be maintained.

The fourth regime represents, then, a difficult arrangement for the major economic powers to accept within the next two or three years. In the short run, it also poses problems for the LDCs to overcome. In the long run, however, it does represent a target worth pursuing. It would preserve Western liberal values better than would the other regimes. It would also offer those governments outside the center of operations of the international economic system a means of voicing preferences, fostering political and economic objectives, and gaining the benefits of both economic stability and continued economic growth, thus preventing them from feeling that they are being frozen out of the evolution of the international system. The fourth regime would be superior to the other regimes in providing political stability in a world that is becoming both more interdependent and more pluralistic.

Selected Bibliography

GENERAL POLITICAL ECONOMY
Olson, Mancur, *The Logic of Collective Action,* Harvard University Press, Cambridge, Mass., 1965, 1971.

APPROACHES TO INTERNATIONAL POLITICAL ECONOMY
Liberal
Bergsten, C. Fred, Robert O. Keohane, and Joseph S. Nye, Jr., "International Economics and International Politics: A Framework for Analysis," *International Organization*, vol. 29, no. 1, Winter 1975, pp. 3–36.

Cooper, Richard N., *The Economics of Interdependence*, McGraw-Hill for the Council on Foreign Relations, New York, 1968.

Kindleberger, Charles P., *Power and Money: The Politics of International Economics and the Economics of International Politics*, Basic Books, New York, 1970.

Marxian
Magdoff, Harry, *The Age of Imperialism,* Monthly Review Press, New York, 1966.

Mandel, Ernest, *Europe versus America*, Monthly Review Press, New York, 1973.

Mercantilist
Calleo, David P., and Benjamin Rowland, *America and the World Political Economy*, University of Indiana Press, Bloomington, Ind., 1973.

Gilpin, Robert, *U.S. Power and the Multinational Corporation*, Basic Books, New York, 1973.

Schmitt, Hans O., "Integration and Conflict in the World Economy," *Journal of Common Market Studies*, vol. 7, no. 1, September 1969, pp. 1–18.

SPECIAL TOPICS
Money
Bergsten, C. Fred, *Dilemmas of the Dollar*, New York University Press for the Council on Foreign Relations, New York, 1975.

Cooper, Richard N., "Prolegomena to the Choice of an International Monetary System," *International Organization*, vol. 29, no. 1, Winter 1975, pp. 63–97.

Hirsch, Fred, "Is There a New International Economic Order?" *International Organization,* vol. 30, no. 3, Summer 1976, pp. 521–532.

Whitman, Marina, "Leadership without Hegemony," *Foreign Policy*, Fall 1975, pp. 138–164.

North/South Relations

Hansen, Roger D., "The Political Economy of North-South Relations," *International Organization,* vol. 28, Autumn 1975, pp. 921–948

Haq, Mahbub ul, *The Poverty Curtain*, Columbia University Press, New York, 1976.

Hirschman, A. O., *How to Divest in Latin America and Why,* Princeton University, International Finance Section, in *Essays in International Finance*, no. 76, Princeton, N.J., November 1969.

Sunkel, Osvaldo, "Big Business and 'Dependencia': A Latin American View," *Foreign Affairs,* vol. 50, no. 3, April 1972, pp. 517–531.

Politics

Aron, Raymond, *The Imperial Republic*, F. Jellinek, trans., Prentice-Hall, Englewood Cliffs, N.J., 1974.

Hoffmann, Stanley, "Groping toward a New World Order," *New York Times Magazine,* January 11, 1976.

Trade

Cooper, Richard N., "Trade Policy Is Foreign Policy," *Foreign Policy*, Winter 1972–1973, pp. 18–36.

Foreign Affairs, symposium, vol. 52, no. 3, April 1974, pp. 437–537.

International Institutions

Camps, Miriam C., *The Management of Interdependence*, Council on Foreign Relations, Inc., Council Papers on International Affairs, no. 4, New York, 1974.

Krause, L. B., and J. S. Nye, Jr., "Reflection on the Economics and Politics of International Economic Organizations," *International Organization*, vol. 29, no. 1, Winter 1975, pp. 323–342.

Index

About the Authors

FRED HIRSCH is professor of international studies at Warwick University. He graduated in economics from the London School of Economics in 1952. After working as a financial journalist on *The Banker* and *The Economist,* he was a senior advisor in the International Monetary Fund from 1966 to 1972. Professor Hirsch is the author of *The Pound Sterling: A Polemic* (1965), *Money International* (1969), *Newspaper Money* (with David Gordon, 1975), and *Social Limits to Growth* (1976). He has been a consultant to a number of official institutions and is the author of several pamphlets and numerous articles on national and international finance.

MICHAEL W. DOYLE is a lecturer in the department of politics at Princeton University and a research fellow in the Woodrow Wilson School's Center of International Studies. During 1975–1976, he taught in the Department of International Studies at the University of Warwick, England. He has recently completed a dissertation on the General Theory of Empire for Harvard University.

EDWARD L. MORSE is a senior fellow of the 1980s Project at the Council on Foreign Relations. His writings include *Foreign Policy and Interdependence in Gaullist France* (1973) and *Modernization and the Transformation of International Relations* (1976). His essays on European politics, international monetary relations, and defense policies have appeared in such journals as *International Organization, Revue française de science politique, World Politics,* and *Foreign Affairs,* as well as in several collections of essays. Dr. Morse has taught at Princeton, Johns Hopkins, and Columbia universities.

WILLIAM DIEBOLD, JR., is a senior research fellow at the Council on Foreign Relations.